I am going to string those moments like melting moons of freshwater pearls on a necklace, and I am going to wear them for Thanksgiving.

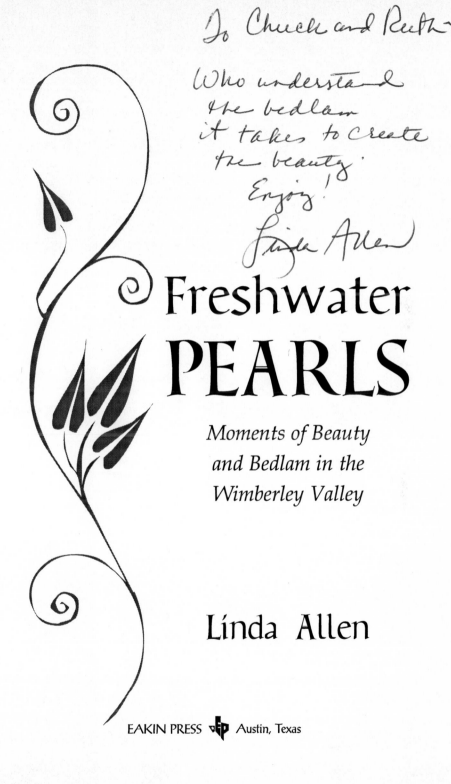

To Chuck and Ruth—

Who understand
the bedlam
it takes to create
the beauty.
Enjoy!
Linda Allen

Freshwater
PEARLS

Moments of Beauty
and Bedlam in the
Wimberley Valley

Linda Allen

EAKIN PRESS ◆ Austin, Texas

FIRST EDITION
Copyright © 2002
By Linda Allen
Published in the United States of America
By Eakin Press
A Division of Sunbelt Media, Inc.
P.O. Drawer 90159 🖅 Austin, Texas 78709-0159
email: sales@eakinpress.com
🖳 website: www.eakinpress.com 🖳
ALL RIGHTS RESERVED.
1 2 3 4 5 6 7 8 9
1-57168-743-2

Library of Congress Cataloging-in-Publication Data

Allen, Linda.
    Freshwater pearls : moments of beauty and bedlam in the Wimberley
valley / Linda Allen.–1st ed.
        p.   cm.
    ISBN 1-57168-743-2 (alk. paper)
    1. Wimberley (Tex.)–Social life and customs–Anecdotes. 2. Country
life–Texas–Wimberley–Anecdotes. 3. Wimberley (Tex.)–Biography–
Anecdotes. 4. Allen, Linda, 1955–Anecdotes. I. Title
F394.W62 A45   2002
976.4'888–dc21   2002015316

Dedicated to
Malone and Cameron
Jimmy
Mom and Dad

Contents

Preface

When my friends asked me to collect my essays for this book, I was paralyzed. How could I go back years and piece together a tumultuous past that somehow threaded its way to the present? How could I call back all that I had left behind and make any sense of it?

But technology has mixed blessings, and the computer has an impartial memory, when it works. After much persuasion and persistence on the part of my friend Dorey Schmidt, I pulled together all the words I could find from the last decade of writing and dumped them in her lap. She has helped me string them together, these irregular moments, creating a picture from the past in which I finally see a pattern.

These moments are a balancing act. Strung across the span of ten years, they are not an exercise in chronology. They are an exercise in living.

I wrote these essays when I was a feature writer for *The Wimberley View*. Never one to keep a diary, I have found, in rereading these pieces, parts of my life that might have gone unremembered had I not written them down. I have found realizations that, fresh when I wrote them, have now become internalized.

What strikes me most is the way the past carries its theme into the present, how the need to balance order and chaos, beauty and bedlam, love and anger weaves its path through our lives. It is a path carved from the details of living, from the remembered comments of a child to the play of winter light along the shadows of the creek.

These essays should surface like memories, unbidden and free from the context of time. Strung together, they create a life, a way of making sense of the world.

And the frame for this world is the Wimberley Valley, the slope-shouldered hills and the spring-fed water. It is the embrace of the people who love this valley and anchor their lives into its landscape. It is my family and my memories of how it all happens.

Many thanks to Dorey and to Linda Bingham for their unflagging belief. Thanks to Angela for her attention to detail and her sense of perspective. To *The Wimberley View* for allowing me the space and the opportunity to write. And to my family and friends for listening over the years to the many stories and for allowing themselves to be a part of them.

Directions

I have lost myself in the best of places. I have lost myself in the worst of places. Maybe you know the feeling. You look around and suddenly realize you're not where you're supposed to be, and, to top things off — you don't know where you are.

I was born without a sense of direction, a deficiency I think I inherited from my father. In his sixty-five years of traveling the globe, he still doesn't know how to get to where he's supposed to be going, but gets there nonetheless. The man can get lost on his own street, but, oddly enough, always ends up in the right place at more or less the right time, albeit short on underwear sometimes.

I've found excuses over the years, and mostly they sound good, verging on a recognizable edge of logic. But that's all they are — excuses — and I know it. I tell myself it's because I didn't learn to drive until I was nineteen, that I was too caught up in the beauty of the landscape to pay attention to landmarks, that the world had changed since the last time I passed that way. And it's all true. But the truest of the true is that I have no sense of direction.

I have become so accustomed to the feeling of being lost that I have no problem stopping at gas stations to ask directions, at Denny's, at roadside vegetable stands and the red lights of major intersections. I think the feeling is universal, although some people admit to it with more ease than others.

I admit to it as if it were my middle name and have found

that, when I walk into a place, a complete stranger, throw up my hands, and confess to utter confusion, the world around me becomes friendlier. People want to help. They've been there. They've been lost at the base of unfamiliar trees, on tangled roads. They've stood at the fork of a mountain trail and wondered which path would take them to a higher altitude with a view of the world, and which would lure them into uncharted territory. They've rocked in the seasick waters of disorientation, stumbled through a language whose words were familiar but made no sense.

When I step into their neighborhoods with the shivering aura of a displaced person, they recognize the opportunity to steady that fear. They draw maps, give detailed directions, replete with a graceful ballet of hand movements signifying turns I couldn't follow if I had to. Sometimes they even offer to lead me, and sometimes, when I'm on foot, I let them, following behind with the grateful gait of one being pulled from darkness to light.

But usually I thank them and try to follow their directions, stopping in the next few blocks to ask again.

I've learned several things from the process, and one of them is that some people don't know where you are, either, much less how to get you where you want to go, but they will give you elaborate directions to your destination, perhaps adhering to the old adage—No matter where you go, there you are.

I got lost in the Department of Public Health building in Austin not too long ago. First I got lost trying to find the place, but that's another story. When I finally did find it and asked directions to the room with the water sample kits, I was given a series of directives about turning left and turning right and swinging doors and exit signs. I did all that and ended up in a lab where everyone was wearing masks but me. It didn't look like the water lab, and they looked at me over their quarantine masks with wide eyes.

I explained to them that I was lost, and their eyes smiled. From behind the masks came a jumble of directions, and their gloved hands swayed like the hands of Thai dancers as they detailed rights and lefts through the maze of the Health Department building, escorting me out of their enclave all the while.

Free of the quarantine lab, I began wandering again and wandered into several wrong departments until one kind gentleman explained to me that nobody really knew where anything was outside of their own department, except for a privileged few, of which he was one. He would take me to the water sampling department, and he did.

Miraculously, I made it out on my own.

I remember, as a child, making the long summer pilgrimage from California to Texas in a car rife with struggling siblings. Picture the scene: early morning, the edges of dawn pulling at the eastern sky, which is pearl melting into pink. We are strangely silent, a car full of sleepy children and determined adults. My parents had a plan. They would haul us through the Arizona desertland in the cool of the morning before we had a chance to realize we were back on the road again.

By the time we had found our voices, we would have covered miles and miles of heat and repetition. In those days of cross-country travel, my parents were devotees of guidebooks that routed travelers through the most interesting back roads, the least-known detours, the most scenic byways.

In the dark of the motel parking lot, lit by the station wagon's headlights, they had found a small road that led off the main highway, cutting the base of a rough triangle that, by suggested proportions, lopped about thirty miles off the trip and took us through a less-traveled countryside.

We set out in that early light on a road that was more or less paved, but that grew less paved as we clocked the miles. I remember staring out the windows with a kind of numbness, inured to the desert landscape after several days in it. Mainly, I remember the roses in the sky and the quiet as the day bloomed before us. I had the impression we were driving through someone's ranch. The landscape seemed more personal than the vistas from the highway.

As the pavement receded, the road grew narrower, and I felt a kind of mounting tension in the front seat where my parents sat. It was the wordless kind, unarticulated, formless, but it tightened into some shape with the shrinking road. By then, we were committed. We had passed enough stunted cactus and low, sloped dunes that turning back would not only imply mis-step, but defeat and a lengthening of roadtime that made the adults feel foolish. So we drove on down the dirt road until we met the sheep.

Imagine this: Imagine all the sheep in the world flocked to-gether and bumping along in a bumbling, tumbling, rumbling cloud of desert dust. Maybe we heard them first. I think we had the windows cracked to save on air-conditioning and gas mileage, and I think I remember the distant motor of sheep hooves revving up in the distance like unpremeditated thunder. What was it, we wondered, scanning the sky as it took on the blue of daylight and drought.

When the sheep came, they came in masses. I've never seen so many sheep—before or since—and they were headed for what was left of our shortcut, so we stopped to let them pass. They seemed to pass for hours, and they redefined my thoughts on sheep. Gone were the visions of fluffy clouds of white wool. Mary's little lamb bore no resemblance to what passed in front of our car, to that bleating, blithering flock of stained livestock.

I think we smelled them before they arrived, a lanolin stench permeating the arid, early air. We watched them in amazement. They seemed to come from nowhere, like the tumbleweeds that sometimes lodged themselves under the front bumper of the car. They seemed surreal, a dusty desert vision that had no end.

We rolled up the windows and turned off the motor, and my parents began to laugh. Not loud laughs, but snorted breaths, snickers, giggles. We started to talk, we children, pulling our-selves upright, demanding to know where we were, what was going on.

My parents pulled the worn map from the glove compart-ment to check the road again, and there we sat right in the mid-dle of it, right where their fingers pointed, as lost as we could be, surrounded by the white water of stampeding sheep.

We all got the giggles. Visions can be ethereal, and visions can be absurd. There in the dust and roses and laughter, we verged on the absurd, heightened by the feeling of being alone in the universe, a family stranded in time, accompanied only by the world's population of sheep.

Really, it was a painting, had we had an artist in our giggling group. Indians with blankets and shepherds' crooks wandered among the sheep, attempting to guide them through a life oblivious to sense and order, attempting to head them in the same direction so the woolly wave did not turn back on itself, a swirling whirlpool of confusion. The appearance of our car probably didn't help, but they pressed onward, mute and impenetrable, as if we did not exist.

And then, as suddenly as they appeared, they were gone, although it took a while. The thunder dissipated with the dust cloud and the silent Indians, and we were left parked on what no longer remotely resembled a road, much less a thirty-mile shortcut, lost and, for the moment, loving it.

We found our way off that road, eventually, with two hours tacked on to the timesaver. We still remember that incident, and we still laugh, lodged as it is in the family archives.

More recently, I traveled the back roads of the Hill Country with a friend whose lack of a sense of direction rivals mine. So bereft were we of moorings that we carried an open map in our laps and referred to it frequently. Even so, breezing through the late afternoon of fall, of gay feather and broomweed, of the declining haze of faded summer, breezing along in a small, sporty convertible, feeling invincible and as found as the glory of a season can warrant, we noticed that, headed as we thought we were for Sisterdale, there were no more hills.

My friend pointed it out in puzzlement. "I don't think," he said, "that we're in the Hill Country anymore."

We weren't, and suddenly I remembered seeing, back in Bandera, a sign that stated "Hondo."

"Hondo?" he said. "Oh, no, not Hondo."

Hondo, it turns out, is not on the way from Bandera to Sisterdale. Some might say it's considerably out of the way. But, fortunately, all roads lead to Hondo, or almost to Hondo, and about two miles outside of Hondo, we turned left and toured Castroville and San Antonio on the way back home.

The point is, we made it home, despite our concerted lack of direction, and all we had to show for it was more wind in our hair and a late supper.

Disorientation is not a disease. It can shake the breathing a little, rearrange the furniture of the mind 'til the real world becomes a sleepwalk. It can take you through landscapes you might never have seen had you known where you were going. And it can make the trappings of home seem most welcome.

Driving into Wimberley, I felt safe, as if I were back in my own closet, although there are days when I figure I could get lost in there if I turned out the light.

Wimberley Time

The lady from Wimberley moved among the stacks of CDs at the music store in San Marcos looking for one special piece of music to give as a Christmas gift to her niece, who had recently braved the foaming white water and soaring red cliffs of the Grand Canyon.

She was looking for *The Grand Canyon Suite* by Ferdinand Rudolph von Grofé, a piece of music that soars as high and magnificent as the canyon itself, that broods and tumbles and sears in the sunlight. She thought her niece should know the magic of the music, since she had slept in the magic of the canyon. She is a lady who believes in the grace and timelessness of classics, no matter how old or how young they might be.

But she couldn't find the piece, searched the racks of classical music and found it missing. So she asked a young clerk, who had never heard of it. *The Grand Canyon Suite*? He scratched his head. Never heard of it. Who's the group?

Another clerk, whose tastes must have run along a more sophisticated or eclectic track, overheard the conversation and offered her assistance.

The lady from Wimberley was dressed in denim and wore sensible shoes. She had, in her lifetime, lived in colder states and on foreign ground, dressed in silks, traveled in circles where she nodded and smiled to languages she did not understand, knowing that the nod and the smile overcame the barrier of words.

She had learned to eat raw fish, eel, sautéed kidney, the sweet blue fungus that grows on corn.

And she had come back with her husband to settle for part of the year on the gray-and-cream limestone of the Blanco River, familiar territory, land she had known all her life.

The clerk glanced quickly at the older woman, then told her who had composed the piece of music, mispronouncing the name in the process, and where she could find it.

Did the lady ever go to Austin or San Antonio? she asked.

Yes.

Which one did she visit more frequently?

Austin.

The clerk began to detail the environs of Austin, describing Guadalupe Street, the Drag, until the lady raised her hand politely to stop her. She knew the Drag, she said. She had gone to the University of Texas.

The clerk's mouth dropped open in shock.

"But," she said, "I thought you were from Wimberley!"

Let us not forget the origins, the ghosts of the land on which we live. They follow us still.

I've heard stories all my life about early Wimberley folk and how they terrorized the more dignified and civilized realms that lay on either side of them.

To their west was German country—New Braunfels, Fischer, Blanco. The Germans, it seemed, had a different view of things, a different kind of work ethic, raising crops in their fields of dirt and plowing through land and life with a Germanic earnestness unmatched by their neighbors to the east.

Don't misunderstand. The Germans knew how to have fun, and they liked their beer and liquor. A man could make whiskey legally in Comal County, while Hays County maintained a veneer of piety that eschewed the legal manufacture or sale of alcohol. The story goes that a certain rancher who lived up near Devil's Backbone in the general vicinity of Wimberley enjoyed both cooking up and consuming the wild juice. The problem was that he lived on the wrong side of the county line.

When the revenuers came to check him out, he explained to them that he thought he was legal. Yes, the still was in Hays

County, but the water came from Comal County. They contended the alibi didn't hold water, no matter where it came from. He spent some time in jail.

To the east of Wimberley lay San Marcos—bastion of academia and intellect and the pretensions of southern hierarchy bred in high cotton country. San Marcos had black, fertile dirt in its fields. It had Victorian mansions with ballrooms on the third floor, doctors, high schools, and the Coronal Institute (pronounced "Carnal" Institute), which later became Southwest Texas State University. San Marcos was on the way to both San Antonio and Austin. It was the county seat and boasted a domed courthouse.

Floating between the earnestness of these two communities was Wimberley, made up of hardy settlers of British and Irish stock living in a kind of never-never land, where time dictated a different clock from the one that ticked in most of the rest of the world. Many might argue it still does.

The thin, alkaline soil in the fields of Wimberley grew more rock than cotton, although the Wimberley family did, at one point, run a cotton gin. The thin soil and sparse grass were more amenable to goats than cattle or horses, although some of the Wimberley men made a living out of rounding up the loose longhorns left over from Mexican herds scattered during the Civil War and driving them along the Chisholm Trail, which ran from South Central Texas to the feed lots of Kansas.

Wimberley folk had a work ethic, to be sure. They just didn't have much to work with, and the ethic was driven more by necessity than the niceties of cultured society. Flood and drought wreaked a devastating havoc on the beautiful land. Limestone stunted the bounty of crops. Industry took the form of chopping cedar, making charcoal, running goats across the rocks.

Such a climate led to basic priorities—food, shelter, clothing, and, in a land that was on the road to no place in particular, human companionship.

Those basics determined the tenor of life in Wimberley, which was made up more of the manners of farmers and country folk than the gentility of the Deep South.

In short, Wimberley had a reputation. It still does.

People who chose to live here were inspired by a fierce independence. Many might argue that they still are. Life wasn't easy. It consisted of back-breaking work and the strength of the fingers that dug into the thin soil because they meant to stay.

Wimberley folk were viewed as rough, as tough and uneducated, although education was always important here. In 1889, the local school claimed 300 students and operated proudly under the name of the Wimberley Academy, run by John Henry Saunders, who was appointed county superintendent of public education in 1907. But by the 1940s, grade levels fluctuated between eighth and tenth grades. Anyone aspiring to a higher level attended school in San Marcos, where they were viewed somewhat dubiously as the country kids from Wimberley.

Many of those kids from Wimberley who finished school in San Marcos went on to college, but the reputation remained unshaken.

"Wimberley was viewed as the sticks by San Marcos people, and probably that viewpoint is still held by people who have never been west of the Balcones Fault," says one San Marcos native living now in Wimberley, who, in the interest of protecting his best interests, prefers to go unnamed.

Keep in mind, he stresses, this viewpoint was "coming from an elite, highly intellectual community with an institute of higher learning where LBJ got his education."

Wimberley was hard to get to, a destination in itself, being on the road to nowhere in particular, and riddled with steep hills, pot holes, and characters like Kim Tinney, who carried rattlesnakes in a bag, walking barefooted from Wimberley to San Marcos, to sell his bounty. He slept in a hole in the riverbank, wrapped in burlap, and occasionally surfaced at local dinner tables to keep the wild tales alive.

Wimberley was peopled with a type of folk who loaded their families into wagons once a month and made the long haul to San Marcos for supplies. It was their one outing, and when San Marcos saw them coming, it locked its womenfolk and children in the houses and watched through the shades as the families camped out in front of the courthouse and the carousing began.

When the Germans held their dances at Fischer, rumor has

it the young men from Wimberley burned streaks in the road with their horses' hooves as they flew through the nights to reach the dances, and then, liquored up with the legal brew of Comal County, burned deeper streaks on the way home.

Hard work begets hard play. Life must hold its balances. Wimberley had its own work ethic, and it ran on its own time— hence the term "Wimberley Time." Basics were always met, but 'coons and possums lurked in the hills, and fish finned the clear waters. A man couldn't be blamed for taking time off from his life to go fishing or hunting. Still can't, it seems.

In 1925, my great-grandfather commenced work on his Wimberley vacation home, hiring local stonemasons to fit the jigsaw of rocks that became the summer home I remember. He paid them a dollar a day, 25 cents more than the going rate, and found himself confronted by an angry cadre of residents complaining that he was ruining the wage scale. He replied that any man not worth a dollar a day was not worth the work he was paid for.

Twenty years later, his son hired the same masons and their sons to add on to the house, which by then had become a crazy quilt of individual rock styles. They built the upper reaches of the sprawling old house, alternating work days with fishing and hunting days.

It was wartime, and the men who weren't overseas worked regular daytime hours at Gary Job Corps in San Marcos for the war effort. Masonry was a spare-time vocation, as were fishing and hunting. Sometimes the masons would disappear for days so they could squeeze in their hunting and fishing. They always returned to the job, and they were always up-front about it. Fishing and hunting were as important a part of their lives as the work they did for money. It was why they lived here. It was the life they chose.

Visitors and newly arrived summer residents had a hard time understanding the attitude that compelled such freedom. Still do. And if the understanding doesn't come with time, they usually move on, stymied, instead of freed, by "Wimberley Time."

Others sought that freedom, saw this valley as a free-floating space between a creek and river—never-never land, a tangle of contradiction and peace. If Wimberley harbored an uncouth spirit, that spirit inspired artists. If it threatened with sparity, it beckoned with liberty. If it changed daily, some things remained the same.

It was always hard to get to, demanded an effort to arrive, an effort to stay, an effort to leave. Still does.

When invited to Wimberley recently for an evening of good company, food, and revelry, a friend from Austin replied, "Oh, Wimberley's so hard to get to, such a long way away. Why don't you come on into Austin?"

The road to where you want to be can be tortuous to folk who don't want to be there, and peopled in the strangest of creatures. The ghosts of its creators abound.

When the music store clerk queried her customer in puzzlement, "But I thought you were from Wimberley," the lady smiled that smile that transcends foreign languages, lifestyles, cultures, and levels of education.

"Oh," she said, "but I am!"

 Cows

Sometimes you find out through the process of elimination what it is you were not cut out to do.

I held the calf with one hand by the rope around her neck, my other hand gripping her flank. Around me, the other calves milled and mooed, shouldering each other and the fence and the cowboys, mud underfoot from the night's brief rain, a faint spring breeze in the air, redolent of stockyards.

"Get your knee under her," said Lyn Holubec, trying to explain the connection between leverage and the art of throwing a small cow on the ground. "Lift her on your knee and flip her. Don't try to wrestle her to the ground. She may look small, but you'll never get her down. She's strong."

I got my knee under the heifer, which wasn't hard—she was small, but my knee was shorter—and tried to lift. Somehow, the connection between my knee and the calf didn't adhere to the concept of leverage. She wouldn't lift, and my efforts to flip her were useless. Lyn was right: I couldn't wrestle her to the ground, either.

"Get your knee under her," said Doc Jones, standing behind me.

"It *is* under her," I said. "I've got short knees."

That's when it hit me. I wasn't cut out to be a wrangler. My knees are too short.

But I kept lifting, and I did finally throw her to her side,

13

holding her down while the crew notched her ear and swabbed her with a purple antibiotic. The job done, I stood up to some friendly back patting and figured I'd thrown my cow, until Lyn decided a few cows later that I ought to try again.

I tried to demur. There weren't that many small calves, I pointed out, and Doc had already laid claim to them, self-proclaimed small-bovine specialist that he was. I was only an observer and had no intention of moving in on staked territory, but Doc willingly granted me one of his small calves—the larger calves going to Mike Park, an Austin firefighter and rattlesnake chili chef.

It was one of those macho things. I couldn't say no, so I grabbed the little cow by the rope, hooked my hand up under its flank, slipped my knee under its belly, and lifted. It was a good effort, but the calf stayed put and turned its wide brown eyes on me in bemusement. The other calves milled into the back corner of the pen and watched the action, not unlike the audience at a black comedy.

The cowboys watched, too, grinning, taking a small breather while I hoisted the little black cow on my knee a few times and finally onto its side. When the second one landed after a few tries, they even congratulated me—"Good throw! Nice throw!" I secretly checked out the height of my knee to see if it was getting any taller. Or maybe I was just getting better at throwing cows.

The second one was a heifer, too, which I was glad of, as the heifers had a little easier time of it than the baby bulls, holding on to more of their body parts, as it were.

(The parts don't go to waste. Mike Parks plans to fry them up for his family reunion on the Fourth of July.)

When the ear was notched and swabbed, I stepped back, and the calf lay there, unwilling to rise. I was afraid I'd hurt her, and bent down to help her up, but she righted herself, tucked her front legs under her, and looked up at me with her dark brown eyes. I stroked her head and told her she could get up, encouraged her even, but she lay there while I stroked her head and blinked her dark eyes at me, even put her head on my short knee.

I looked at the cowboys. "What do I do now? Take her home?"

They were doubled over in laughter.

Finally she unfolded her legs, stood up, and meandered out of the corral. I decided I'd had the ultimate experience in throwing a cow, told Doc he could have the rest of the little ones, and settled back to watch a curious rite of spring that occurs on cattle ranches right about the time the bluebonnets crowd Texas roadsides and the peach trees bloom their pink blossoms.

It's roundup — time to separate the calves from their mamas long enough to separate the bulls from the heifers, long enough to turn the bulls into steers and notch the ears so the wranglers can tell them apart on the range and in the milling dust of the cow pens — left ear for heifers, right for steers.

It's a noisy operation, and, had it not been for a brief and long-overdue rain the night before, it would have been a dusty operation. But it's been going on for generations on one of Wimberley's largest ranches where, in those springs with more rain, the grasses roll down from the Devil's Backbone to the Blanco River, and the cattle stud the green fields, herds of black and brown Brangus scattered among the wildflowers and oak trees.

Pal Wenger, like his father before him, keeps the rocky hills and the sprawling fields free of the cedars that plague what once was open space in Wimberley, moving the cattle from pasture to pasture for better grass.

Except that this year, it's been a little different. This year, with almost no rain since October, there's precious little grass in the fields, and this year, for the first time he can remember, Pal is culling his herd in the springtime, letting go of about 20 percent of them because he doesn't have the grass to feed them.

His cowboys are an eclectic crew made up of his foreman, Lyn Holubec; Doc Jones, a media soundman; Mike Parks, firefighter; Marcella Hager, daughter of the late Lloyd Leinneweber, who was Wenger ranch foreman for twenty-two years; Roger Hager, her husband, part-time cowboy, full-time lens specialist; a retired air force general from San Antonio; and a retired executive with an interest in cows.

Some of the crew have a background in animal husbandry. Some just grew up on a ranch or around cattle. Most of them have nothing to do with cows 364 days of the year but would trade almost any activity for a chance to immerse themselves in the sweat and grit of roundup.

As the mud and the jokes fly, and the calves squirm, and the cows bellow, Pal explains that most of the hands return every year to help with the roundup. It's hard, dangerous work, he says (and I nod as a larger calf pulls Doc Jones through the mud on his knees), but once that cowboy blood starts in the veins, it runs the body like a good cow pony, and they can't get enough of it.

"These guys come and help mostly because they get to ride their horses and push cows," says Pal.

"It's something different," says Lyn Holubec of the ranch work. "It's always something different. You're cutting hay, riding fence. It's something people don't do much anymore." He laughs. "Probably for a reason."

Mike Parks grabs on to an even larger calf, clearly enjoying the challenge, and flips it almost onto its other side. Pal laughs, shakes his head. "Mike doesn't know his own strength. Instead of a 90-degree flip, he'll do a 270."

And while the work is intensely physical, Lyn Holubec explains that the crew takes care not to rile the cows any more than is necessary to get the job done.

"The easier we treat them, the easier it is to handle them now and in the future."

Marcella takes a moment from her job as the antibiotic swabber to explain that roundup gives her a chance to actually do something on her horse, to use its skills for the very purpose for which they were honed. Marcella was born on the Wenger Ranch and lived there 'til she was seven. She grew up surrounded by cows and the people who work them, and though she works for Hidalgo, Inc., in her real life, she still dreams of open ranges and a fast horse to cover them.

"I'll take off any day to do this kind of stuff," she says, adding that the way they do it on the Wenger Ranch—riding the pastures to round up the cattle—is becoming a kind of anachronism in the cattle industry. These days, with the exception of some of the ranches in Wyoming and Montana, most cattle ranchers herd their cattle with helicopters. A way of life that has inspired a whole genre of folklore, music, and literature by its very physicality and closeness to the earth is rapidly falling prey to the efficiency of technology and its distancing effects.

"This," says Marcella, nodding toward the cowboys wrestling with the cows, their horses tethered to the fences after the morning ride, "is about as close as you get to the real thing."

Still, some things have changed. In earlier days, when Marcella's father ran the ranch, the hands would arrive in the dampness of early light to smell lunch stewing in a cauldron near the corral. When noon rolled around, Lloyd would dish out the stew—often made from a raccoon he'd shot a few months earlier and stored in the freezer 'til roundup. These days, when the crew breaks, it's for a quick run up to Casa Blanca and a round of Jose's enchiladas.

When the calves were taken care of, the crew shifted its attention to the cows, shooing them into a back pen, then herding them one at a time into the squeeze chute or stock where the hands check the numbers tagged in the cows' ears, and Pal checks his list to see if it's a cull or a keeper.

The cows he's culling, he explains, either calved in March, aborted a calf in the spring, or are older cows.

The cowboys herd the keepers into the squeeze chute, then punch them with pesticide eartags to keep the flies away, shots with vitamins for fertility, worming medicine, and vaccines to prevent the sexually transmitted diseases that can occur when a bull jumps the fence.

"All of this is what gets to be known delicately as animal husbandry," says Pal, opening the gate to let another cow charge through.

He leans back against the pale green and gold lichen, the rough gray wood of the cow pens, and nods his head back toward the dry fields and distant hills that border his ranch. This is the worst he's seen it in at least twenty years, he says. Letting go of the cattle in the springtime is not an easy decision, but buying hay is expensive, and the whole cattle industry is hurting.

Pal—and many other cattle ranchers—are hoping that the mad cow disease that terrorized England and made Americans dubious about foreign beef will provide some relief for the low prices in the U.S. beef industry, but so far, that's pure speculation.

Lyn tells the story of the farmer who took his calves to market and paid more to feed them for three days than he could make on them at the auction, so he decided to give them away. He took them into town with some feed and water, a temporary pen, and a sign for free calves. When he came back the next day, he found three more calves in the pen.

A cow charges into the chute, kicking at it like an angry five-year-old. She's a cull and charges out of the chute, running into the wrong gate head on, time and again, until Lyn coaxes her back into line and herds her into the other pen. Cows, says Pal, are not known for their intellect.

As they bellow to their calves and kick at the chute, Pal acknowledges that, to many people, the process seems rough, inhumane. But, he says, it's a necessary part of the beef industry, and it's been going on for centuries.

Pal's participation in it actually benefits the area. The Blanco River runs through his ranch, unaffected for long distances by development or septic tanks, and his ranch provides much of the uncluttered vista that gives this valley its character.

"This sort of arrangement is why a lot of people moved here," he says. "If it works out that I cannot devote a lot of acres to ranching, a lot of people are going to miss it."

And so are a few cowboys. There's a hard-hitting but congenial sense of teamwork going on here. The men and Marcella work together with the seamlessness of people who know what they're doing and enjoy it, which is probably why they keep coming back year after year, taking time off from their jobs to ride their fine horses across the springtime landscape, circle the ropes over their heads 'til they sing, and grapple in the mud or the dust with the cattle.

It's an old rhythm, an old romance. It may be going the way of a changing time, but some flames take a long time to burn out. And some never do.

 # Heat

I lay in bed about a month ago, late-night, windows open to the sound of the creek, starlight sifting through the cypress, waiting for the breeze.

It never came. Something was different in the night. With no air-conditioning in my bedroom, I had been reveling in bringing the outside in, and the night air was soft and redolent of creek water and honeysuckle. Cicadas had started their echoing hymns in the trees, singing the summer over and over again. Frogs bellyached alongside, disgruntled basses in an acoustic choir.

Up until about six weeks ago, a breeze played at the windows 'til in the night I would reach for the sheet, maybe the blanket, and pull them loosely over me like another layer of sleep.

And in the mornings—in the mornings, the world felt like the first spring. If the night air had been soft, the morning light was softer, something I could almost inhale and carry inside me, at least through the first round of morning duties—Cheerios, clothes for the children, missing socks, mismatched shoes, a constant eye on the clock, and the push out the door with broken phrases that snagged us each morning, like "late for school," or "late for work," or "if you don't get in the car now ..." (That one always dangles ominously because I seldom know how to finish it off.)

But about six weeks ago, the breeze stopped. I lay in bed and waited, not realizing what I was waiting for, reading late into the night, waiting for sleep to blur the pages, and waiting for something more.

Finally, I closed the book on my own, turned out the light, and turned in that loose cocoon of heat to find a cooler stretch of sheet. It wasn't there, and still I waited for sleep and something more.

When sleep finally came, it was fitful. I kicked the sheets from the bed and thrashed the pillows. I woke in the night and turned the overhead fan up, riffling the pages of magazines beside the bed. I pulled my hair from my damp neck and grabbed at sleep again.

In the morning, the light seemed stale, as if it were a remnant from an earlier afternoon from which the sky had leached a bit of its blue, tired and a little disaffected.

I realized then what we all know now. It's damned hot. Some might argue—This is Texas. This is summer. Would you have it any other way? But somehow, as Texan as we are, we waken every summer with amazement to that first serious heat, and we turn to one another with puzzled looks, put our hands to the back of our necks, and say in aggrieved and outraged voices—"It's hot!"

Of course, people not acclimated to the heat might have complained earlier, when the mercury began its invasion of the 90s, but we wait 'til it closes in on 100 before we start to carp.

That's when it begins to aggravate. Getting in and out of the car becomes a chore, and, with the sweat beading on foreheads and upper lips, we fight back the urge to fight back at small annoyances. If the heat is out of proportion, so is the rest of the world. Everything annoys, and coolness is the only antidote.

Sometimes even air-conditioning won't soothe the savagery that lives inside the heat, and I try to drown it in the creek, which does well to change my perspective as long as I can stay immersed. Something about the shock of that cool water closing over me jolts the heat, turning it to memory until I get out.

And it's dry. It hasn't rained in weeks, it seems. We forget how last June we wrung our hands every day when the rains came, when the winds blew the tree branches into the sides of our houses and hail threatened our cars. We forget how we glued ourselves to the Weather Channel, praying desperate prayers that the 40 percent chance of inclement weather wouldn't spoil our wedding reception or birthday party or picnic.

Now we'd welcome the rain, welcome the smell of wet caliche, the dog's muddy pawprints as he pads through the kitchen and shakes his great shaggy coat with joy.

It rained a few weeks ago. Remember? And briefly, after the splurge, that breeze found its way back, drifted like a long, cool scarf through the trees. We draped it over ourselves, felt it quicken the energy as we breathed deeper breaths, trying to take it in, make it last longer than the evening.

We grow almost indifferent to the heat if we aren't outside in it, learn to stay inside, brave it only in short trips to and from the car, trips that seem intensified by the shock of the temperature change.

And yet, we should remember, there can be a cleansing in the heat. I've lain in it for hours in younger, lazier days, when soaking up a tan seemed as important as a child's needs or a work schedule does now. I've felt the riverbank beneath me, a scaly hot limestone, while the sun seared above. There was a kind of purification going on, along with the sunburn.

I've worked in my garden in the early morning, only to find that the heat had sneaked in while I was absorbed in caging a tomato plant or weeding a row of beans. I would always press it as long as I could 'til, red-faced and drenched, I lost the endurance contest to the stultifying, stupefying heat.

Afterward, when washing the sun out of my system in the shower or the river, I felt a kind of fluid, tired relief. If the heat drained energy, it also washed away some buildup of pressure, of anger or frustration, and I felt lightened, like the whiteness of a sheet hung to dry in a sky of southern sunlight.

In the winter, when clouds press close and a damp chill permeates all, when the children stay inside until it appears as if a toy bomb has exploded in the house, when all is gray and seems it will always be that way, something stirs inside.

Heat burns a memory. Clouds may obscure it. Cold may swath it in the necessary layers of wool and feathered comforters. But in the damp, mud-caked days when rain slides past the window forever and the chill has nothing to with the mercury level, but goes past the bone to some deeper longing for sunlight, dreams of summer stretch and turn their lazy, heat-drenched bodies in repose.

We know they'll waken. We even remember our fierce denial of those days in August or late July. But we still stretch out our arms. After all, this is where we choose to live. This is Texas.

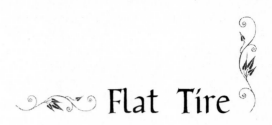

Flat Tire

Some things get you started thinking on coincidence.

I know people who don't believe in the phenomenon. Every serendipitous circumstance is a function of divine intervention, no matter how minor or miraculous. What some call coincidence, others see as God's way of paving a road so rife with potholes it can be undriveable at times. It is a force beyond us that pairs the unlikely with the unforeseeable, and if the pairing is fortuitous, we offer prayers of thanksgiving. If not, we beg for strength and understanding and the will to go on.

Others see that force as a random sense of humor. Life is a long strand of coincidental pearls that we can rope around our necks as many times as it will go. We move through each day driven by luck — good and bad — no more, no less than that. To attach a greater significance to coincidence is to layer our lives in superstition.

Two extremes: one reaches for prayer; the other, for the horseshoe and the four-leaf clover.

I probably fall somewhere in the middle. Some days are so steeped in prayer that I can't even spell coincidence. Other days plow through luck or the lack of it like a late-night poker game.

The other day I fell susceptible to a wonderful case of either divine intervention or the headiness of sheer coincidence, the kind that makes you want to shake your head in amazement at the way the world lines up for roll call.

23

I was on my way from work up to St. Stephen's to pick up my children from school and take them to pitch practice before I picked up a pizza for them to eat before I took them to AWANAs. Time constraints were closing in, and the familiar riff of *not enough time in the day* was making the rounds in my head, so I decided to turn on some external music.

It worked for a few miles. The twenty-year-old jazzy softness of Mark Almond sifted through the scratched recording, and I was singing along to the strains of *I don't want to go, I don't want to go, I don't want to go back into the city* when I felt something bump the back tire of the car. Intrepid driver that I am, I kept singing and rolled another half-mile or so up the road before the roar reached me.

When I couldn't hear Mark Almond anymore and was having a hard time hearing myself, I settled back onto the pavement of Farm Road 3237 and realized that something besides my life was out of kilter. It was my car. I knew that roar. I'd heard it before. I had a flat tire.

Let me set the scene. It's springtime in Wimberley. The skies are a gunmetal gray, the promise of moisture hanging in damp threads of late-afternoon torpor, and I've never changed a tire.

As a woman in the '90s, that's a hard statement to make, but confession is good for the soul, they say, and I've been accused of being dragged, kicking and screaming, into the twentieth-century. (The American car, as we know it, is a twentieth-century invention.)

The last flat tire I had was a little over a year ago. I was driving back into town on the Blanco highway, about two miles from my point of departure and five miles from Wimberley, when my car gave a little hop and listed to one side. I knew immediately what was wrong and pulled off the shoulder of the road, or what would have been a shoulder on any other road, the problem around here being that we have too many shoulderless roads.

I stepped out of the car and looked at the unmistakable low of a flat tire and a car leaning off the incline that passed for a shoulder.

I took a deep breath and decided that, no matter what, I was

going to need my spare tire. Even if I didn't know how to put it on, I could at least dig it out of the trunk, which was a considerable undertaking in itself.

As I wrestled with the tire and my own lack of practical experience, a truck pulled up behind me and an older man stepped out. At first I froze, and all the lectures, headlines, and scary stories danced through my head in one swift blur. Sunlight blazed overhead, and Wimberley's fields burned green and blue and gold with wildflowers: a juxtaposition of beauty and senseless fear.

He stuck out his hand. "Looks like you got a problem, little lady," he said. "I'd sure hate to see my wife stuck out on the side of the road with a flat. Let me help you. The name's J. D. Whisenant."

I relaxed. I knew the name, knew his sons, felt some comfort in familiarity. Mr. Whisenant studied my car for a while, pulled a jack out of his truck, a jack out of my trunk, and began working on the precarious job of lifting the side of my car without tipping the car over into the shoulderless ditch I had all but pulled into. Twenty minutes later, I was back on the road after heartfelt thanks to Mr. Whisenant.

I felt I'd been pretty fortunate, and whether Mr. Whisenant was another pearl in the long string of coincidences I could call my life, or whether he was an answer to whatever prayer I was no doubt breathing at the time, was something I didn't give much thought to.

So the other day when I heard the roar, it was with a sinking feeling. I pulled off onto the gravel behind a truck, which was pulling into a driveway, and got out to inspect the tire. It was flat as the sense of adventure I feel when confronted with mechanical difficulties.

The truck I had followed off the road was bumping over a cattle guard, and I could see an older man getting out to shut the gate.

"Sir," I called with embarrassment, "I've had a flat tire. Could you help me, or do you have a phone I could use to call someone?"

He looked up from under the brim of his gimme cap, and it

was J. D. Whisenant, a year later and eight miles away from my last flat tire.

I had to laugh. Of all of the people in Wimberley I could have followed into their driveway ...

Mr. Whisenant didn't remember me until I jogged his memory a little—different vehicle, longer hair, different road. But the tire was just as flat.

He was, I told him, my guardian angel of flat tires. He laughed at that, shook his head, and proceeded to climb under my van to take a look at the spare tire. He hammered on it for a while and pried at it with a wrench before asking me if I had an owner's manual. I did, and after that it was easy.

While Mr. Whisenant was under my van, a friend drove up and asked if she could help. She picked up my children at school and took them to their ball practice while we wrestled with the tire.

The sky was still gray and the air still damp when Mr. Whisenant tightened the last lug nut, and the cows were lumbering up from the ravine to watch the goings-on. This time, no wildflowers blazed from the fields, because the cows had probably eaten them all, but still some juxtaposition hovered there, hard to put into words, the quirk that makes us wonder at coincidence or breathe those quiet prayers.

Still, it's almost enough to make me a believer. What, after all, would you have the guardian angel of flat tires look like? Would he wear a flannel shirt and tennis shoes, a gimme cap and the beginnings of a beard? Would he tell you stories about his wife, his son in Nashville, his grandchildren? Would he gruffly brush your comments aside when you apologized for your wealth of impracticality? Admit that he liked chocolate cake?

Horseshoes and clover aside, as I headed past the cows on my way out, steering clear of their placid contempt for cars, for pumped-up tires and women of the '90s in distress, I said a quiet prayer, thankful for, if nothing else, the boon of coincidence. I can recognize two beliefs in one prayer.

Think about it. We live in a good place. I'm baking Mr. Whisenant a chocolate cake.

Beauty

About a month ago my eight-year-old son, Cameron, found me in the kitchen, pulled me away from my work, and made me listen to him.

He had a surprise for me, he and his Granny. His brown eyes widened to contain the surprise, and I knew that all I had to do was give him a little push and he'd let me in on the secret. It was bubbling at the edges, scenting the air with suggestion.

He gave me clues. It was something for my garden, something that would make the garden prettier. I gazed through the doorway at the gathering of clay pots overflowing with passionate purple petunias, golden cosmos, and small, deep blue clusters of something that Cameron says remind him of tiny lightbulbs.

My garden is a glorious tumble of beautiful chaos. The basil grows amidst the dianthus. The tarragon peeks through the coreopsis. Without the time to devote to a garden planted in the ground, I have taken immense comfort in the profusion that flows from the clay pots outside my door.

"You'll like it, Mom," Cameron said. "Granny and I picked it out. It's a gift for you and me."

But they still had to get it, he said, and when Grandpa picked him up from school the next day, they would bring it to me.

Surprises demand control from an eight-year-old, but he had it. He kept the doors shut on what he knew.

The next day, his grandpa picked him up from school, and they arrived at the house with boxes. Cameron handed me the first box, which contained a wrought-iron plant stand. "It's wonderful," I told him. It would hold one of my pots beautifully, give it a little height, which is always a plus in a garden.

But he had more, and he came into the house carrying another box. When I opened it, I found myself holding in my hands a large, delicate glass bubble that was meant to fit into the plant stand. I turned it in amazement. Iridescent, it bent the world around it to its sphere and magnified the pinks and blues and growing greens 'til they ran together like oil on water.

It reminded me of mornings spent on a deck, blowing bubbles into the soft air. They would hang and drift on nothing, the rainbows of the world sliding through their surface until the surface thinned to holes and they joined the air that held them.

Here was a permanent bubble, a solid memory from childhood of those fleeting globes on which the world slid so freely.

"Do you like it, Mom?" he asked. "It's called a gazing ball. I thought it was so pretty. I thought you would love it in your garden, and it's ours."

"I love it," I told him. "I love it, and I love you."

I held this redheaded child, who is growing faster than I can feed him, in my arms, and told him how much it meant to me that he and my mother had taken the time to pick out a thing of beauty and place it where I could look at it every time I looked out my door.

I tried to tell him how much I needed that, but he is easily bored with abstract explanations and goes straight for the heart of the beauty, which in this case was the sliding colors of the garden against the iridescent glass of the gazing ball.

He was right, on so many more levels than he could articulate. His heart understood the need for beauty in a world where the colors seem to be sliding more and more into black and the darkening gradations of gray.

We hear the terms *gratuitous violence, gratuitous sex, gratuitous profanity,* and I would like to add *pain* and its accompanying *misery* to the list. Those are the commodities for sale in the cult of the ugly. Those are the products of ennui and atrophy, of disillusion and the ultimate cool.

Those commodities drive the soul of movies and headlines. They influence clothing and language. They needle the core of anger in our hearts 'til we are angry at the world and unsure why.

This is an age that could use a little gratuitous beauty to balance the colors. This is a time that could benefit from more beautiful surprises.

I remember a dinner party one night when we played a kind of survivalist game after the meal. What ten items would you take with you if you were one of the last people on earth going to live on a primitive island with handful of other survivors? The answers were both predictable and personal. Laden with tools and sacred books, seeds and ropes and family photos, the lists painted pictures framed in practicality, desperation, and sentiment.

The list that has stayed with me was the least specific and the most controversial. One of the guests, a lovely, soft-spoken woman whose artwork and demeanor had turned more than one head, said that she would bring nothing practical with her through that keyhole at the end of the world. She would bring the ten most beautiful objects she could find.

She looked around the room at the guests vying for the most resourceful list and said she trusted them to supply the island with practicality. She would nourish the battered souls. Without beauty, what was the point?

Over the years, I've thought of her list. When the movies I see litter the screen with disposable bodies, and the core of humor is grounded in profanity, I think of that list. When the headlines and lead stories dwell on violent death, both because it is the appalling reality and because it sells the story, I think of her list. When the music crashes around me, and I can't and don't want to understand the reason or the lyrics, when the musicians say the whole point is noise, I think of her list.

Beauty is a relative term, even a cultural term, but some forms transcend differences. Some forms speak to dreams and longings that never quite go away.

I had a young friend who lived with us who had adopted a spiked hairdo, Doc Marten shoes, holey jeans, and a vocabulary heavily laced with profanity. She was a beautiful young woman battling her way through adolescence in a media-driven world where beauty is synonymous with the ghostly pallor of drug addiction and anorexia.

I was bemused by the whole thing and tried to remember that my miniskirts and hip-huggers, the hair that obscured my face, my pale, almost white lipstick, perplexed my parents.

Then, one evening, I found a heap of tousled blue netting on the counter in the bathroom. I held it up, and a splashy, romantic ball gown unfolded before me. The bodice was sequined and seductive, and the long skirt was a cloudy swirl of sky blue netting. It was beautiful in a fairy princess way, the kind of gown I used to play dress up in, a gown rescued from the racks of a thrift shop to dress up some young girl's dreams.

I knew that dress. I'd worn it in fuschia and gold and scarlet and black, in satins and laces and diamonds and pearls. I'd worn it in ballrooms, on moonlit balconies, in the back paths of gardens scented in sandalwood and gardenias. I'd worn it in all my young dreams of a beautiful life, in all my fairy tales, and when I saw it heaped on the counter, I realized that someone else had been trying on her dreams again, trying to see if they still fit.

Those dreams change shape as we grow older. I would wear a different dress on that balcony now, but it would still be beautiful, and I would still seek out the scent of sandalwood and gardenias.

We need those pockets of unearned beauty. We need the visions that blaze out of the darkness, both real and imagined. We need to remember the ones that illuminate our past, and we need the gift of new ones.

Too often, we see only lines of traffic and billboards. We see only the rules that apply to practicality and the red tape of living in an overpopulated world. We are the victims of bureaucracy and disillusionment, and we wrestle and reason with the cult of the ugly and come up empty-handed and brokenhearted. We back off. Sometimes, we give up.

Beauty makes the world resonant. Ugliness is a wall. It is the color of pain. It is the music of violence. It is the high style of absurdity.

This is a plea for gratuitous beauty. Something unexpected,

without justification, a surprise that defies the groundwork of reason. We need to give it to each other—to our children, our parents, our friends. We need to give it to strangers, too.

The morning after my son's gift, I sat on the front steps at daybreak with my coffee and watched the world wake up. I saw it first in my gazing ball. It came in softly, riding on the feathers of low, sketchy clouds. It came in pinks and golds and mother-of-pearl, and as the half-light washed the sky, it painted the flowers of the garden into the globe.

It was magical. It was a gift of love. It carried me through the day. It was wonderfully, unreasonably, and downright beautiful.

# Goldfish

L et me tell you a story about fish and hamsters and not about turtles.

About six weeks ago, my children's father gave them two goldfish and an aquarium for the goldfish to live in.

It should have been a good dream, and maybe, when all is said and done, it will be, albeit a more expensive dream than it set out to be. I remember having goldfish as a child. I remember the small bubble of a bowl we kept them in, the flaky food, the pretty rocks at the bottom, and the castle they flirted in and out of with their golden tails like scarves behind them

What I don't remember very well was the actual cleaning of the bubble-like bowl. Perhaps my mother, in her infinite patience and infinite (or so it seemed) blocks of time, cleaned the bowl. That was not part of the dream.

And then, too, I remember my younger brother's goldfish experiment, in which he and my father filled a large green glass jug with gravel, water, aquatic plants, and several goldfish. It was a dramatic presentation, to be sure, but they had shielded themselves well against ever having to clean the container, since there was virtually no way to get the contents out of the jug once it had been filled, short of dumping it out the small mouth of the bottle. And then, you could see before you even tried that the aquatic plants would pose a barrier there, so it didn't seem worth the effort.

We all watched that bottle with interest, my mother's interest bordering on extreme skepticism. Maybe she had cleaned too many fishbowls to have much faith in the ability of the spindly plants to provide enough oxygen to keep the fish alive or the green glass jug clean.

Well, the green glass gradually grew greener, and the spindly plants flourished in the green light and thickening water to the point that my mother made my father and my brother carry the jug outside to the back porch, where it stayed as long as I can remember. It carried its own aroma, I recall, a kind of musty fragrance redolent of backwater and swamp.

As for the goldfish, amazingly, they lived longer than goldfish should, I think. It was hard to tell, since the jug took on a kind of green opacity that discouraged goldfish viewing, but every once in a while, I could see a mysterious, rich glint of gold burn its way through all that dense green. Truly, it was amazing.

So when the very small aquarium, replete with ceramic castle, turquoise pebbles, plastic plants, no aerator, and two very large goldfish arrived at my house to live one day, I had more than mixed emotions.

My first thought was that the goldfish were oversized for the aquarium. They were, my boys told me, Dad's leftover striper bait, and their names were Cameron and Goldie. It wasn't hard to tell which child had named which fish. The three-year-old's name is Cameron, and the six-year-old has more sense at his age than to name striper bait after himself.

Without an aerator, my friends informed me, I would have to change the water frequently in order to keep the fish alive, which would involve pouring sufficient tap water the night before, letting it sit to rid it of chlorine, switching the fish ... it was more than I had time for or wanted to hear about.

The boys were ecstatic. They each had their very own pet, and although we have a big, gentle, soft dog who follows my children everywhere with a kind of resigned faith, they still needed something small to cup their hands around and call their own. I was just hoping that they wouldn't try to hold the fish and wondered how many tears would flow with the fish's eventual demise.

Well, Cameron the fish, a sort of mottled brown-and-gold

fellow, didn't make it long at all, barely twenty-four hours. I explained to his puzzled namesake that he might have been an old fish who needed to move on to heaven. We buried him in the side yard in the cactus bed, and it wasn't too traumatic, because we still had the brave, bright flash of Goldie, who had actually settled down into a spot he cleared of gravel behind the castle.

Malone, my oldest, fed him carefully and flew into rages when Cameron or one of his young friends dumped quantities of fish flakes into the water to sate Goldie's delicate appetite.

So when Goldie eventually gave up—and he lasted a long time, to my way of thinking, several weeks—the loss was harder to take. There were tears on Malone's part and anger when I tried to explain that the fish wasn't living under optimal circumstances. He had grown to love the fish, and, too, there was the loss of ownership.

We buried Goldie beside Cameron the fish, and later I learned that Cameron the son had secretly dug up Cameron the fish to see if he had gone to heaven yet. I don't think he found much, which leads me to believe that something else might have dug up Cameron first.

Malone, and then, of course, by power of suggestion and the order of birth, Cameron, were both distraught. If they couldn't have a fish, what could they have? The dream was turning bad.

Well, I hadn't been keeping up with the legal status of pets, so I suggested we get a small turtle. Again, I was digging into my childhood for memories and coming up with these small, maybe three-to-four-inch turtles that used to come with brightly painted shells and plastic palm trees. I remembered that pet advocates had objected to the painting of the shells, but I thought we could still find the little creatures in all their natural beauty.

They were fun, I told the boys. You could hold them and marvel at their turtle-traits, their retreating heads, their tiny, clawed feet. They didn't require an aerator and could live comfortably in the aquarium, which would require very little water and cleaning.

We all got real excited about the turtles.

Malone accompanied me to the pet store in Austin, and while he browsed the tarantulas, scorpions, and striped monitors, perhaps creating dreams of his own, I looked for the little turtles. There were none. I found exotic turtles that were much larger and more expensive than I had in mind. (I was looking for cheap. The fish, after all, had started out free.) I found all kinds of lizards and snakes and birds, but no little turtles.

So I asked the "pet consultant" who was minding the store. Henna-haired, with one earring and combat boots, he laughed at me. I must have seemed archaic and dusty. Clearly, I wasn't up on turtles.

"It's not legal to sell those anymore," he said. "They carry salmonella."

"Like chickens?" I asked.

"Like chickens," he said. "Especially if you don't clean their tank very often."

"Oh."

So we bought a hamster. Those and the gerbils were the least expensive mammals in the store, and they were living in cages that looked very much like our aquarium except they had wire over the top.

Hamsters, said the pet consultant, were not as high-strung as gerbils, and I could see by looking that they were fluffier and didn't have the long, rat-like tail that will break off a gerbil if you hold it by its tail.

"Get a baby," the pet consultant said. "You can train them to be nice. Maybe it won't bite as much."

That floated loose another memory of me as a young girl, standing beside the hamster cage with a bloody finger, crying, the hamster scurrying madly through the kitchen, and my mother torn between my finger and catching the mad hamster before he lost himself in the labyrinth of the house.

We picked out a small, fluffy, tan-and-white hamster, and Malone named him Kyoochie—or something to that effect. After we had bought cedar shavings, hamster food that Malone insisted looked like bird food, a water bottle, and a water bottle holder, the pet consultant put Kyoochie in a box for us and instructed Malone not to open the air holes or the hamster would gnaw his way out.

We had quite a few stops to make, so the hamster accompanied us to Central Market, El Lago, Sam's Club, and Target. We were afraid to leave him in the car. It was too hot. In

Central Market, a lady at the neighboring counter regaled us with hamster stories, not the least of which was the story of the hamster that got loose in the house and subsisted on the edges of curtains and rugs and the odd shoe kicked under the bed.

(That appeared to be a recurring theme as people told us their hamster stories—sort of like the fish that got away. Everyone has a hamster story to tell, and it usually involves the one that got away.)

That same lady reached over solicitously and, before we could stop her, punched out one of the air holes because she thought the hamster needed to breathe. We cringed, but the damage was done.

Well, the pet consultant was not a pet consultant for nothing. By the time we got to Target, Kyoochie had gnawed a hole large enough to get his head through, and when a hamster can get his head through an opening, you can count on the body following its lead.

So, after a story from the cashier about the hamster that got loose in his house, we were able to get an extra bag, into which we transferred the hamster. The bag made it almost all the way to Wimberley before Kyoochie discovered a weak corner and gnawed his way through it.

By the time we got to St. Stephen's School to pick up Cameron, Malone had transferred the hamster to a hard hat he found in the back seat, and that seemed to contain him for the moment.

At St. Stephen's, the children gathered round, fascinated, but a little afraid to touch because Malone had discovered on the way home from Austin that Kyoochie was prone to biting, a habit I hoped we could wean him from.

We took Kyoochie home that night, cleaned out the aquarium, lined it with the fresh smell of cedar shavings, stuck the water bottle to the wall, and put Kyoochie in his new home. As I was fixing dinner, Malone came in to show me the furnishings he had installed in the aquarium, which consisted of a couple of small buckets, the ceramic castle, and an engraved silver dish to eat out of.

As I mentioned before, the aquarium is small, so very little room was left for the hamster, and one of the buckets was tall enough that the hamster could climb it and get out, so we re-arranged the living space. I also substituted a jar lid for the silver dish.

Satisfied that the hamster couldn't get out of the aquarium, the boys and I covered the top with a towel (we didn't have any wire mesh) and went to bed.

At five the next morning, my distraught six-year-old awakened me to tell me that the hamster was gone. And gone he was. Still is. I looked under the bed with a flashlight, plowed through a seldom-used closet, pulled furniture away from the wall. We even put the aquarium in the middle of the floor with food and water and small steps leading up to the lip to facilitate the ease with which Kyoochie could reenter his home, although apparently the little thing has suction cups on his feet and doesn't need much help climbing walls.

All to no avail. Disappointment and grief reigned in our house that day. Malone kept trying to figure out how the hamster could have possibly climbed the aquarium walls, while Cameron cried.

I took a deep breath and promised a new hamster, privately gritting my teeth, wondering how we had moved from no aquarium at all to a lost hamster in the house and promises of a new one.

But this week Malone and I traveled back into Austin and bought another hamster. This time, I took another deep breath and bought a hamster habitat—a modest one, but one that was made for a hamster and offered no avenues of escape. The bonus here was that if I paid the $25 for the habitat, I got the hamster free! Malone was impressed to no end.

I also bought an adult hamster, hoping he wouldn't bite. Again, this hamster made several stops with us in Austin, but we made sure he was in a chew-proof box. We were learning.

Malone decided to stick with the name Kyoochie but then switched it to Ralph, explaining that Ralph was a nickname for Kyoochie. He's since gone back to Kyoochie because he has a hard time remembering Ralph.

Kyoochie's a nice hamster. Maybe we got it right this time. We've only lost him twice, and that was in daylight hours when we knew he had to be in the same room we were in, and we've found him both times. We've had him two days, so the future is bright for the present.

He's sweet. He lets the children hold him upside down, toss him out onto the bed, and pull him out of the habitat tunnels. Occasionally, when they let me hold him, he snuggles into the crook of my arm and lies very still. Everybody needs a breather.

I have to say, I was getting soured on the dream as I watched the tears flow, but now I'm not so sure. Kyoochie is soft. You can hold him in the palm of your hand, and he doesn't bite. I think that means he likes us, and the dog's not jealous.

There's a lot to be said for all that. It was a circuitous route getting there; we still haven't found the first hamster; but maybe the dream's still a good one. I think we'll keep it.

Grandmom

My grandmother had red hair. In later years, it lightened its flame as a bright fire goes to ash, but it was only the surface flame. The inner flame never cooled in my grandmother.

That flame was her trademark, in a way, her signature, her nature. For the first sixty years of her life, it may have surrounded her head like some halo of fire, but mainly it burned inside, a red-hot, intelligent pride that bent for only the most human of reasons, only the most quaking intimations of the heart.

My grandmother died last month. It was a difficult passing in some ways, a smooth one in others. She was ninety-two, bent over, reconciled mostly to a wheelchair, although occasionally she used a walker, and the red hair had lightened to white. She suffered at the end from Parkinson's Disease, from the grueling equations of years of arthritis, from the many ailments of aging, including a good mind that encompassed the knowledge that so much of what she loved had gone before her. In some ways, that may have hurt the most.

At first, while watching her passage from this world to another, I was so caught up in trying to justify her leaving that I never really thought about the final effect of departure, as if packing the suitcase or arranging the flight route was the net worth of the trip itself.

Finally, of course, it's not. Finally, the effect on those left behind is absence, clear and simple, an emptiness you learn to live with, to incorporate into your life.

When the absence hit, it didn't matter how she died or whether it should have happened differently, with more medical assistance, a prolonging of the end. It mattered only that she was gone, and the absence simply gaped

Not one acquainted often or intimately with death, I looked for ways to skirt the hole, a kind of circling denial that doesn't work. Finally, I cried, which helped, and then I started telling stories, and that helped even more. Absence is a hole that cannot be skirted, but I'm not sure it can't be cushioned, and I have found the most enduring, the most comforting cushion to be the memories.

My grandmother was a teacher, an ambitious woman who loved children and believed fiercely in the sharing of knowledge. She taught for years in San Marcos and, until the day of her death, couldn't shop the aisles of the local grocery without at least one former student stopping her—"Mrs. Williams! Do you remember me? You taught me in sixth grade forty years ago!"

And chances were, she did remember.

She took time with her students. Many credit her with their later successes in life—her belief in them, her enthusiasm, her unwillingness to let ignorance override intelligence if there were any intelligence there to fight it.

She taught me, as well. She taught me many things, but since she captured my family's presence only in the summer, it was not schoolwork that she taught. It was life and it was fishing.

She loved to fish, and I do, too. She dragged me and my brothers and sister all over the banks of the Blanco, the San Marcos, and the Cypress, looking for deep holes shadowed with rocks, for the still waters beneath overhanging trees, for the eddying pools at the base of falls. She could read water. She could smell fish. She knew how to find them.

She taught me to thread a worm on my hook before I was old enough to be squeamish and took me with her in the early morning to dig the thin worms from her black garden soil. If we were desperate, we would buy worms, the plump, sluggish kind—one to a hook. Her worms were wiry and feisty—maybe three to a hook—and the whole thing looked like Medusa's head when we finished baiting them. Irresistible, I always thought, to any fish.

We first fished with cane poles. They didn't get as tangled and were easier for a young child to maneuver, although I remember well the frustration of trying to edge that pole through dense underbrush to reach a choice destination.

Even with cane poles, lines still tangled with each other, with the trees, with the bottom. My grandmother was patient, a trait necessary to fishermen, and untangled all our lines, but she was also competitive. Being a child shielded no one from her competitive spirit, and it became the family joke that if you turned away from your fishing spot to thread your nice-sized catch on the stringer and rebait your hook, you would come back to find Grandmom fishing in your spot, and, being grateful to have been included in the first place, there was not much you could say.

In later years, the tables turned. My brothers, sister, and I spent much of our fishing time untangling her line from trees or, more often, from itself. It seemed only fair.

I remember when we graduated to artificial lures. We were fishing out on the old farm on which Grandmom had once raised her family, casting our lines into a large tank surrounded by trees that leaned their languid branches over the murky water in some frozen frame of a gnarled ballet. If there were any music in the still summer air, it was the low bellow of bullfrogs along the banks.

My grandmother reached into her rusty green tackle box and pulled from it a handsome thing—a shiny lure with bright, dancing rubber bands jiggling on its sides. It would catch bass better than worms, she said, and that water was ripe for bass if it was ripe for anything.

I could tell she prized the lure, so I tied my barrel knot carefully, making extra loops with the monofilament to ensure it gripped the lure tenaciously. Then I searched the sloping bank for a suitable bass hideout and settled on the low-hanging branches of a tree, its leaves dabbling in the water like indolent fingers, water skeeters scooting through its shade.

I cast carefully, aiming underneath the branch, and managed to hook the main limb solidly, as if the lure had just found its purpose in life. This was no catch-and-release situation. The lure would not let go, and as I fiddled with the line, it broke, leaving the lure in the tree and the line floating on some nonexistent breeze.

My choices were to climb the tree and retrieve the lure, or lose it.

The tree wasn't that high, but it hung well over the swampy water, and I didn't like the looks of it. My grandmother watched me keenly as I tried to decide, and I knew that, as a true fisherman, I really had only one choice. So I climbed the tree.

All was well until I saw the snake wrapped like some wrestler's bulging arm around the limb that held the lure. Swampy water was one thing. Snakes were another. I froze, eye to eye with the python, then backed out of the tree in half the time it took to climb it.

"There's a snake up there," I panted to my grandmother.

She shrugged. If it wasn't black, she said, it probably wasn't poisonous. I was just a little more frightened of the snake than I was of my grandmother, though, and I refused to climb the tree again, offering instead to buy another lure.

In the distance on the far side of the tank, we could hear gunshots as a young man blasted away at bullfrogs. My grandmother called to him, inviting him to untangle the snake from the tree with his gun, which he obligingly did. As the bullet opened the side of the snake, it dropped from the tree into the murky water, pushing up against the lure as it fell and knocking it into the water.

"Just go on out there and get it," my grandmother said. I looked at her in amazement and slowly shook my head. I think I offered to buy her a new lure again, and I think, in the end, she refused me and offered up a coffee can of wriggling worms, and we got on with the fishing. So much for artificial bait.

My grandmother was tough and strong and loving. While I always suspected she liked boys better than girls, I also knew she expected the most from me, and I tried to show it to her. She owned a set of World Book Encyclopedias and encouraged me to take the heat off summer afternoons by lying on the floor and reading them. When she died, she left the set, perhaps a bit outdated in some areas, to my eight-year-old son, in whom she had a great deal of faith.

She believed in naps every day, a structure I couldn't fathom (I do now), and made my brother and me lie on either side of her in her big bed during the afternoons. Convinced I could never sleep in the middle of the day, I tossed and turned in a rebellious heat until I melted into it. Always, she put me on her left side, and when I questioned that, wanting to trade places with my brother for reasons that escape me, she explained that she put me on the side closest to her heart. It was a good answer. It carried a lot of water for a long time. I guess it still does.

Sometimes, at night in the summer, she would unfold her old army blanket on her lawn, and we would lie in the dark and name the stars and listen to the crickets and the whip-poor-wills. She was dismayed when the City of San Marcos installed a streetlight near her house. Always in favor of progress, that was one light she could have done without.

She took us to Aquarena Springs in the summers and glided with us in the glass-bottom boats while we all dreamed of catching the six-foot catfish we saw beneath us. She took us swimming in the Aquarena pool and Rio Vista Park.

She came to California, where I grew up, to visit sometimes, and I remember how she and my grandfather would walk together through the garden, touching the leaves of the plants, peeling back the skins of the oranges to that bright, wild juice inside. They loved the coast of any ocean, and my grandmother could put away more crab, shrimp, and oysters than most people can dream of.

When I left California for college in Dallas, I came down to San Marcos and Wimberley for weekends, and she and my grandfather would welcome me and my friends with an open bedroom and the ultimate comfort food, buttery milk toast, for late-night snacks.

The whole floor of my college dormitory awaited the care packages she sent me—pounds of foil-wrapped fudge and coffee tins of, not worms, but chocolate-chip cookies and spicy cheese biscuits. I would find notes left in my refrigerator to the effect that someone had "borrowed" some fudge and left a token bite of something else in return. My grandmother healed the homesickness of a whole floor of freshman girls.

When I moved back to Texas after graduate school, she took ill, felled by a massive infection that lodged itself in the hip she had scheduled for replacement. She turned a shade whiter than her glorious hair and lay in her hospital bed in Austin with her eyes closed and the flame burning so low it was hard to see.

Newly graduated with an esoteric degree and no immediate job prospects, I sat by her bed and held her hand, read her the newspaper and parts of novels (she was an avid reader), and watched TV with her. Gradually, the flame strengthened, and she began making requests. Would I bring her some shrimp next time I came? A spot of sherry?

We watched Reagan sweep the country in the presidential elections, and, nonpolitical myself, I was amused to see the fervor with which she embraced the newly elected, having once been a fervent Democrat.

When she came home from the hospital, she ran off everyone who tried to take care of her with her desire for independence. No one could dictate my grandmother's life but herself. Logic has no hold on independence, and the sheer strength of that flame burned her right through her illness and out the other side, emerging a medical miracle, of sorts, whose only complaint was that one leg was shorter than the other.

We became a team. I had the time, and we both needed the company. She taught me so much about older women, how some loves, no matter how frivolous, never leave us. We shopped together, and I loved nothing more than her delight in a new dress. I learned that at twenty-five, when I looked in the mirror and saw someone much younger, at seventy-seven, she looked in the mirror and saw a sixty-year-old who still boasted a head of flaming red hair. She chose vibrant greens and golden oranges that spoke of the dreams of a younger woman, and I applauded her gift of a young heart.

I learned that she was proud of me, that she loved the woman I had become, and that she was inordinately proud of my two sons—of all her great-grandchildren. It was knowledge that has helped build the flame in me.

We lived close by, and until life circumstances forced

change, we visited frequently, taking her to lunch, a span of four generations among us. She watched my oldest son when he was a baby, and she sat in my kitchen for hours, helping me peel peaches for summer cobblers. We shared recipes and gin and tonics. She sat in the shade while I gardened and called out advice wrung years ago from the soil. She taught me how to love the black-eyed pea.

Her pride never flagged. At times, it could be annoying. Bend, I'd want to say, bend and accept some help. But she wanted to live alone after my grandfather died and continued to do so until she died. No one wanted to buck that strength of spirit.

There are so many other stories, so many details left out of the telling. She was thorny and beautiful as the roses she trained in her garden every year, willful and lovable as the wire-haired terriers she kept in her yard.

And she was so strong.

After she died, my parents and my aunt and uncle divided the treasures of her house among the family members. Knowing my older son's love of learning, she left him her encyclopedias.

Knowing my love of food and cooking, she left me beautiful plates and platters, but perhaps the best of her gifts that I am just now unwrapping is the flame. I feel one burn inside me when I need it most, and I'm learning that it's fed by a pride and a strength I think I have drawn through the generations from her.

To my youngest son, she left one of her most striking gifts. He cannot go anywhere that people do not run their fingers through his wild curls, shake their heads in awe and envy, and say, "Where did he get that hair?"

I have only one answer:

"My grandmother had red hair."

Rope Swings

The other day reminded me of what I used to think summer was.

Late afternoon was hot. With an unreasonably mild July behind us, summer has hit with a vengeance. We have been spoiled, coddled by the cool breezes that swept through on some aberrant cold snap that rendered most of July as likable as a late-spring day.

But that's all in the past now. This is the real stuff of which summers are made. This is the heat we brag on. This is triple-digit macho heat, if you believe my thermometer. This is time to hit the creek.

So yesterday in the late afternoon, my boys, my sweetheart, my puppy, and I loaded ourselves into the car and set off for one of my favorite swimming holes—Scudder's on Cypress Creek.

I grew up in that deep spot, probably learned to swim there as much as anywhere. Scudder's is a wide spot in the creek, banked at one end by a dam, so the water pools in a cool, gentle swimming hole, deep enough to catch the bodies of the children hurtling through the air from the rope swings that dangle from the limbs of the cypress trees that shade it.

A family that has been friends of my family—both sides—for four generations now owns Scudder's. It's an old-time swimming hole, opened to the neighbors and the neighbors' dogs. When we arrived at 5 P.M., the grounds around the creek, stomped solid by bare feet, were filled with wet dogs and children in bathing suits. Grandparents sat on the dam at the far end and watched, a slight distance removed from the splashfest and the spontaneity that water breeds in children.

My group clustered in inner tubes not too far from the steps, soaking in the water that makes you forget the sweltering accumulation of the day's heat. We sipped on cold drinks that beaded the sides of the cans and glasses, and we lay back in the black, patched rubber tubes as if they were elegant lounge chairs in a leafy salon.

With my puppy in my lap in the inner tube, I watched one of my boys climb the rungs of the ancient cypress to reach the swing, watched him catch the rope as someone heaved it back and forth in the water, coaxing enough momentum from the swing to throw it into the tree.

Rope caught, the boy leaned back into perfect tension with the rope to maintain his balance and stepped out onto the truncated limb. With a single breath, he launched his body into the air in a wide arc that circled him toward the dam, the far bank, over our heads, and, finally, with the biggest possible splash, into the water.

His blond head emerged seconds later, ringed in watery silver halos that widened and slipped around his neck in concentric circles. Creek water spouted through his grin. He turned a somersault just below the surface, and he swam for the rope, pitting his young body against it as he threw it toward the tree for the next person to catch.

Then he was at the bank, headed back toward the rungs in the tree for another go at the late-afternoon air.

It's timeless, that rope swing. So simple, the interplay of air, body, and water. It is technology at its lowest, and reality at its clearest. There's nothing virtual about that rope swing.

When I was a child, I was scared to death of that swing. I would sit on the bank, fresh from the creek, hugging my shivering body to stay warm in the 99-degree heat, and watch the other kids soar through the summer on that rope swing. The limb was longer then. You could walk out farther on its reach, and I swear it was higher off the ground. (The tree must have shrunk, as things will do when they get older.)

I watched many children attach themselves to that rope and fly with it across the river. I scrutinized their balance as they leaned backward on the limb of the tree, the tension of the rope defining their angle. I watched their wet feet feel along the slick bark of the cypress, and I wondered that they did not slip, and if they were to slip what would happen.

I studied the water directly below the tree, since they would surely fall, and determined it to be shallow near the tree's base, where small sunfish flashed in and out of the root tunnels. I imagined it would be a painful fall, one marked by bruises and concussions and swallowed water, and I marveled at the confidence those children felt in the rope, in the matching of their bodies to the air. I gasped when they stepped off the edge of the limb into nothing and began to fly.

A child on a rope swing is a lovely thing. A child on a rope swing is summer. Tanned and elegant in their fluid bodies, the boys were more beautiful than they would want to know, both daring and goofy, poised for the splash. The girls were like the stems of water lilies, taut and supple and curving to meet the needs of the water and air. They sliced the water like a silver knife, while the boys cannonballed and sent the whole surface into waves of disarray.

They were my friends in the summer heat, but I couldn't share their confidence in the tree limb and the rope and the air. It was in that very tree that I discovered I had inherited my father's acrophobia, a paralyzing fear that defies reason, logic, and love.

I wanted to swing through the summer, too, and I gazed at the line of children waiting their turn, but couldn't join them.

And then one family gathering, my uncle, my father's younger brother, noticed that I was not taking my turn at the rope swing. A professional good old boy, with a soft spot for children, with curly dark hair and blue eyes and a bear hug for everyone, he sat down next to me, tickled me for a split second, then quit because he knew I didn't like it.

Why wasn't I standing in line, he asked. Were the boys too rough? The older kids too mean?

"No," I said. "I don't want to swing on the rope swing."

"And why not? Nobody doesn't like a rope swing," he said.

"Well, I don't," I said.

"I see," said my uncle, studying the tree. Would I like it any better, he asked, if he went up the tree with me and helped me?

I stared at the tree that had held so many children and surely was waiting for me. It had let none slip from its limbs. It had carried them all as if it had arms that let go only when the rope began its wide arc. It was a beautiful tree, I thought, and I knew I wanted to climb it.

So, with my uncle close behind me, I climbed the rungs toward the small platform and the extending limb, climbing slower and slower as I neared the top, until I finally reached it. I wrapped my arms around a small portion of the enormous, shaggy girth of the tree and tried to find a way to make it from the top step to the platform without trusting my sense of balance, which had deserted me somewhere down near the third rung.

My uncle steadied me with his arms, and I clung to them like banisters, studying each freckle, each curling hair, each link in his watchband, studying everything except the distance between me and the water. No sense in dwelling on imminent death.

Somehow, I found myself sitting on the platform, which was small and wet and as slick as the tree limb. My uncle stood behind me and caught the rope swing, which someone in the water had thrown to him. I could swing from the platform, he said. I didn't have to walk out on the limb if I didn't want.

I remember the heavy tug of that thick blond rope in my hands as he handed it to me, an impossible tug, and I handed the rope back to him. He took it. For the next eternity, my uncle talked quietly to me about rope swings and heights and my own abilities. I clung to his stout arm and stared at the sunlight shimmering between the shadows, at the trees on the far side, at the hill of St. Augustine rising in the distance on a slope from the bank. I stared at everything except the water. I even took the rope a few more times and tried my foot out in the inner tube that hung from the end, but I couldn't turn loose.

And then my uncle paid me one of the kindest tributes an adult can pay a child. He put his arms around me and told me I didn't have to go off that rope swing. I could just turn loose of the durn thing and go back down the tree with him. It didn't matter to anybody if I did, particularly to him, and he'd be proud to escort me back down those rungs.

So I did, and when we reached the bottom, he hugged me, told me I was brave to even try, and that one day I would be ready to go off the rope swing, and there was no need to go 'til then.

He was right. It wasn't that summer, but a later one, and I don't even remember shoring up the courage to do it. Perhaps it was one of those things my body learned during the dormant winter, when rope swings hang motionless over leaf-covered pools and children forget about flying.

Perhaps I had more confidence in my body, or perhaps I had learned to manipulate the tensions of the world to create a balance of sorts that allowed me to fly.

But I do remember the glorious spinning air as I sailed off the edge of that limb. I remember soaring through the heat of midday, through the lavenders of dusk and through the star-shot skies of night, after the feature at the Corral Theater.

I remember hitting the water too hard and shoving half of Cypress Creek up my nose. I remember a rope burn when the rope caught under my arm as I let go. And I remember the perfect leave-taking, the rope leaving my hands on the upswing, my toes pointed, my body tensed for the perfect entry into the water, like the ultimate dive.

I have swung from the best of swings, I like to think. I have braved the cypress at Blue Hole and watched the boys on lunch break run across the concrete, shirtless and in wet jeans, to catch the ring. I have positioned myself in midair over empty inner tubes floating by on the Blanco River. I have flown through the air at Little Arkansas, and I have hung, suspended in time, above the waters of the Guadalupe.

Central Texas summers were made for rope swings.

So it does my heart good to see the boys line up impatiently at the rungs on the old cypress. Summer's changed a lot since I was small. Memory paints it as a glorious stretch of idyll, when heat and waiting waters braided time into a seamless fabric that rolled through June and July and August.

Doubtless, I was bored at times. Doubtless, I sang to my mother, "There's nothing to do!" But if I did, I don't remember.

Now, in the haze of work and children, I would welcome an afternoon of lazy boredom. Still, I take it vicariously. When my children sing, "There's nothing to do," I think, *Enjoy it while you can.* Then I pack them up in the car, throw the puppy in the back, and head for the watering hole.

Because nothing chases boredom like a rope swing.

Spring time

Last Monday I woke to a howling at the window, a thrashing in the blinding shards of light that slashed the sky. Rain hit the deck running and slid down the rocks toward the creek like the maddened dash of children toward a summer's worth of water.

It was 2:30 in the dark that is not quite morning, no matter how the clocks insist. It was that timeless hour when the soul is at its zenith because the body lies prone and does not hinder its wild dance, and while my body burrowed deeper into winter's blankets, my soul stood at the window and watched the wind cut through the leafless cypress trees and careen down the path swept clean by the wandering of the creek.

If I did not know the wiles of Texas weather, I would have called that storm a demon, a passionate revenge or grief, a frenzied freedom released from a soil packed hard by the heel of winter's mud-encrusted boot.

But no, it was just springtime knocking at the door.

At 2:30 in the morning, no one listens to reason. No one sighs gently in tune to the strident whistling outside their window and falls asleep to the dream of daffodils and primrose. No one measures the insistence of the raindrops on the roof and at the window, of the water seeking every careless entrance. No one blesses nature's innovation at 2:30 in the morning and feels the earth stretching to meet the growing demands of sweet purple onions or the slender asparagus pushing at the rain-soaked clods, reaching for that cloudless sky.

We lie in bed and shiver at some unease brought on by nighttime storms. We cannot see the wind, but at night we can feel it. We feel it shake the house and bend the trees. We feel the dark tattoo of rain upon the earth as if only the blindness of night allows a glimpse into that world. We are all the same then, in the wild and shattering dark.

So I did not sleep well in that darkness. I listened and tried to breathe the evenness of sleep. I tried not to let the waking dreams pull too hard on memories of flood or devastation. I hummed the lullaby of reason, which could not be heard above the madness of the storm.

But in the morning, in the early wet light of morning, I found that someone had opened the door to springtime's knocking.

We've had a mild winter, everyone says. No glacial suspension of the odd icicle from the eaves. No postcards of the valley edged in silvered air and frost. A few mornings, I cleared my windshield of ice, racking up tardies for my children because I could not drive through the solid curtain of a cold night on the glass. But really, it's been mild. El Niño has thrown its tantrums at the rest of the country with a vengeance we can only guess at or read about, but it has only cried on our shoulder, left us with soggy ground and a perplexing warmth.

Still, we had a winter, a mild one that showed up just late enough to kill ambitious tomato starts and tweak our concern about the Hill Country peach crop, just late enough to point out the arrival of spring.

Because I think that's what that was the other night.

Spring is nature's beauty, and all beauties carry a slight air of unease about them. That is their nature. Springtime is a straining at the edges of a sweatered, zipped-in comfort. It is a call away from the warmth of the flames in the hearth. Springtime says, *Dance with me, sweetheart, in the moonlight, in the sunlight, in the rain.*

Springtime says, *Wear my flowers in your hair. Throw off the safety of your dark gray woolens and wrap yourself in the fine mist of the green that I promise. See the bare branches outside your window?*

Open your window and look for the green. You don't see it? Look again. Tilt your head. See the light misting along the limbs? See how the world welcomes you? See the promise of the future in the rain?

Spring is swollen with promise and passion. That is what was heaving outside the window in the dark of Monday morning, and when I walked outside in the early-morning light, I saw how the season had pushed itself beyond its limits, swelled its promises past the lines drawn by winter.

The skies were scrubbed and cloudless, a blue like I barely remember. They made me hold my breath and want to cry. I walked through the tall, wet grass toward the cliff over the river and smelled the brown surge before I saw it—raw earth and wild onion, surface of dried cedar needles like a skin on the water, twigs, logs, trees. The river was climbing out of its banks, breathing deeper and deeper breaths 'til it spilled over the limestone and covered the stray rocks and the tiny cypress and cedars. It blanketed the stark white land and undulated up the cliffs. "Chocolate milk," my children said. *Oh, yes,* I thought. *Swift brown sugar. Cappuccino. Cream.*

The wind had bent the bamboo that threatens my yard, whispering a leafy takeover like some Japanese jungle. I have tried to cut it, but my boys love its stark shade.

"Look," I say, "it's taking over. Soon it will invade the septic tank or come through the windows. It's devious. It knows what it's doing."

They look at me with their dark brown eyes darker with pity. "Mom," they say, and they pat my arm with their small hands. "Mom. It's okay. We like the bamboo. We don't want to kill the bamboo."

But springtime's wind had bent the larger cane and snapped it so it lay like pick-up sticks amongst the straighter, younger shoots. The hurl of water in the creek had bent the bamboo along the banks to the ground in a fine tangled mess of panda food.

"Wow," said the boys. "Wow."

And sunlight—the sunlight was out of its bounds. It stretched the sky and the bounds of the earth, and I felt myself trying to breathe it, wanting to reach into the dirt of the garden I no longer have, to feel its warmth beneath the earth, to feel it stretch all the boundaries of the senses, because that is how things grow.

It was spring. Spring cleaning. It was a high flute melody, or a pennywhistle, a wild Irish tune about flowers and rash love. It made me want to live in the sunlight all day long and forget all my other promises. It made me want to climb out of my banks.

And I was not the only one. As I drove down the street at midday on my way to some dubious obligation, I saw my neighbor's pig, Buster, ambling down the middle of the road just as lazy and as happy as you please. He had no obligations, and while his yard is lush and green and his fence is laced with honeysuckle and a canopy of wisteria, while he is fed to surfeit with lettuce leaves and carrot shavings, with potato skins and broccoli stalks, while he has deep and luscious mud wallows and shade trees and the pleasant companionship of Iris and Venus, who are pigs of the female persuasion, Buster could not stay in the confines of his life that fine, awakening day.

And so he was ambling. Buster is a Vietnamese pot-bellied pig who had been purchased by the dreams of monetary success. But while ambitions are honest and come from the heart, public taste is fickle and relentless in its pursuit of change. Now Buster's existence rests mainly on the fact that he has an existence and no one can find a good reason to deprive him of it.

He is black, with an impressive overbite and a couple of curly tusks that may serve him as well as a handlebar mustache. He walks mincingly, as pigs will, and his purpose in life that Monday morning seemed to be the other side of the street.

Buster is dependable enough that his owners often let him out of his sweet enclosure to roam the yard, and he obliges by staying in the yard, which has all he could ever need, including indulgent, protective dogs. But on Monday, with the sunlight at its glorious peak, the river leaving its banks, and springtime busting out all over, Buster was springing his prison of ease. He was leaving the yard.

I thought, feeling a little sorry for Buster, that maybe that wasn't such a good idea, so I stopped in at his owners' to tell on Buster. Sure enough, they didn't think that was such a good idea, either, so my neighbor grabbed a loaf of bread, called to her daughter, who was mowing the calf-high grass in her bathing suit, and enlisted both of us to herd Buster back to sanity.

"He never does this," she said, shaking her head. "I don't get it. Maybe he wants the acorns under the oak trees."

I had to laugh. I got it. Acorns were as good an excuse as any and better than some, because if you were a pig, you could always use acorns as a plausible excuse, but really Buster had spring fever and needed to break all the rules, so he just did.

You should have seen us. My neighbor had no shoes on— only socks. Her daughter had on cutoffs and her bathing suit top, and I was wearing an apron. We were standing in sunlight scattered through oak trees and spread across a carpet of acorns. We had sliced white bread in our hands, and we were talking to a pig, who was uninterested at best.

Spring fever has no truck with reason or white bread, and Buster had it bad. Because he is laconic by nature and not given to dispute, he took no exception to our entreaties and demands. He simply ignored us. It was not until we picked up sticks and enlisted the help of the dogs, Belle and Blanche, that Buster acknowledged our presence, and he did it with grace. He lifted his head from the sun-warmed earth and the acorns and looked at our oddly clad, stick-wielding posse. He looked at the bread. He looked at the dogs. Maintaining his dignity all the while, he expressed an interest bordering on indifference in the bread and allowed himself to be coaxed back across the street.

I don't think he was the least bit swayed by the bread. I think he was influenced by the dogs. But I had to admire him: Like the swelling river, like the green pinfeathers bursting from the gray limbs of the cypress, like the gusting and howling explosion of spring in the darkness, Buster had broken his barriers, if only for a moment.

I need to take note: I need to leave my yard, if just for a little while. I, like Buster, need to hold my own, my personal, my sunlit celebration of spring.

Lucy the Cow

If cows dream, it must be of greener fields, of the acres that lie just beyond the fence line, the way we dream of a more exciting life somewhere, a better break, newer love. But when cows close their eyes, they must see the wind move across fields unfettered by fences. They must dream of freedom, of sweet grass and billowing clouds for a landscape.

Lucy was just such a cow, probably still is—a cow with a taste for freedom and the fields on the other side of the fence.

Lucy joined my aunt and uncle's herd of longhorns a couple of months ago, or at least trod the same fence line for a day or two. She was a red Brahma, finely bred, with a lineage that could be traced back to the heat and dust of India, and she had been born and raised for her first eight months on a ranch near Blanco.

She had foot-long red ears that hung like silky pendants, and a soft black nose. Her hump was smooth and settled over her shoulders with the comfort of a fine cape, giving her that characteristic stoop-shouldered stance of a Brahma.

My aunt had long watched the Brahmas on that ranch, had even, with a deprecating humor, wished for one.

"I just think they're cute with their big ears," she would say.

Not often given to indulging whims, she only played with the idea of ownership, but my uncle took it seriously.

My uncle is a longhorn man, drawn to the lore of the trail drive and the open prairie. The horns from his first cow, who died a few years back, hang in his office like some great spread of arms open to the wild range, to the grasses and cactus, the weather.

The longhorns roam his ranch with a placid abandon, munching on first one field, then another. They are not money-makers, he is quick to point out. They are a part of his landscape.

But he was willing to mix up the herd a little, introduce a stranger, if just for the novelty, so he bought my aunt a cow, plunked a neat pile of bills down on Lucy, short for "Lucille Ball," and had her trailered home across the hills from Blanco.

"As we do with all animals," says my uncle, "whether it be chickens or cows, we always pen them up for a period of time."

So my aunt and uncle put Lucy in the cow pen for a couple of weeks to accustom her to being away from her clan. They were not without empathy, though, and understood how it might be hard for a young cow to leave her family and travel to unfamiliar territory, so they gave her a friend. In the pen with Lucy they put Easy, a handsome black-and-white fellow of about the same age.

Easy is as close to being a pet as most longhorns ever get. His mother died in a bog, unable to raise herself up out of the mud after laboring through a rainstorm. Bottle-fed and stroked by the hands of numerous children, Easy is gentle enough, un-afraid of people, and wears the hide of a fancy handbag or west-ern sofa.

The idea was that Lucy and Easy would bond, form a last-ing friendship that would carry them through the fields of coastal Bermuda and the shade of cedar brakes. My aunt and uncle thought they had, thought they could see it in the way the calves hung out together, chewed their cud, ruminated on what-ever it is cows ruminate on.

But, in fact, they didn't.

Two or three days after freeing them from the cow pen into the field with the other cows, Lucy turned up missing. At first, my uncle didn't worry about it.

"Any cow," he says, "when you put it in a new pasture, it will walk the fence."

Maybe, he figures, it's checking out the boundaries of its confinement. Maybe it's looking for gaps.

Lucy, it appears, was looking for gaps, and she found one. With growing concern, my aunt and uncle checked with their neighbor to see if she had seen the calf. Sure enough, she had seen Lucy walking the fence line with a good deal of concentration.

"Then we started looking for her in earnest," says my uncle.

Walking the same path as Lucy, they found the same gap she had found, near the Deer Creek Nursing Home, and, on the other side of the fence, they found Lucy.

Lucy was content on the other side. She had discovered some deer blocks, and they suited her taste just fine. Besides, there were none of her kind on my aunt and uncle's ranch, and, as it turns out, for Brahmas kind is important.

"Brahmas," says my uncle, "are clannish." He didn't know it when he purchased Lucy, but he knows it now. They stick together and do not enjoy the company of other cows. Given their own kind, they will graze together as far away from the other breeds as space will allow. Like the Indian Brahman, for whom they were perhaps named, they have a caste system, and they do not mingle with other castes.

So Lucy had no interest in returning to the ranch. Nothing awaited her there.

At first, my aunt and uncle thought to lure Lucy back with feed, but, ignorant of feed buckets, she was not interested. Then they thought to round her up with horses, but, unaccustomed to horses, she would not round up.

So they called in Lonnie Rodriguez to help. Lonnie is a cowboy who rounds up cattle, shoes and trains horses, cooks a mean piece of meat, looks good in a hat, and works in the movies occasionally. He agreed to help but suggested that first they take Easy out there and see if he couldn't persuade her to return to the ranch.

My uncle looped a rope around Easy's neck and led him over to Deer Creek. With a kind of friendly nonchalance, Lucy ambled back into the ranch with Easy. My aunt and uncle patched up the gap in the fence and thought that was the end of it.

The next day, Lucy showed up on the wrong side of the

fence again. My aunt and uncle didn't call Lonnie this time. They knew what to do. They slipped a rope around Easy's neck and led him over to the nursing home. Lucy patiently followed him back to the ranch.

But this time, my aunt and uncle realized that, with the gap closed, Lucy was jumping the fence, and they decided to put her back in the cow pen for a while. They hoped that, with a little more time, she would accept the ranch as home.

Lucy, however, wasn't interested in returning to the cow pen, preferring instead to linger in a field knee-deep in the green sway of coastal Bermuda. Easy seemed inclined to linger also, so they left them there, browsing through the autumn field together.

An hour later, Lucy was on the other side of the fence.

No two ways about it, Lucy was a jumper, which, my uncle later discovered, was common to her breed. She loved the challenge of a good fence, loved the singing air that raced between her belly and the barbed wire as she cleared it. Maybe there was a headiness to being aloft, if only for a moment, in an unhindered flight to freedom—the cow who could clear the moonlight, given enough of it to fly by.

Jumping cows were nothing new to my aunt and uncle. They'd had one before who could clear a five-foot cow pen fence while hobbled neck to foot. That cow was a dreamer, a flyer who loved the lure of the air more than food.

"It just flat-footed jumped that fence," says my uncle. "Plus it had all the food it could ever eat in there, and it still jumped the fence. Yeah, we ate that one."

But they didn't really want to eat Lucy. She was too pretty, and they didn't think they'd like the taste of her fancy pedigree.

By then, Lucy had grown wise to the lure of Easy, and that lifetime bonding they had hoped would form between the two calves turned into a lasting indifference on Lucy's part. She'd had enough of Easy, wouldn't follow him back to the ranch a third time.

So they called Lonnie again.

"How big is the calf?" he asked.

"Oh," said my uncle, "about 600 pounds."

Man, thought Lonnie, *that's a big calf.*

Lonnie suggested to my uncle that he call Dr. Joe Burke at the Cypress Creek Animal Clinic and see if he could get his hands on a mild tranquilizer that could be put in Lucy's feed to sedate her. The idea, he explained, was that he could get close enough to rope her if he had to, and she'd be easier to handle if she was feeling more tranquil and less independent.

Lucy, however, wasn't hungry for the food they brought. She was happy with the good green grass and the deer blocks at the nursing home, and she turned her black nose up at the bucket of doctored feed. Instead, she took to the cedars and ensconced herself in all that stickery green, which made her virtually unropeable.

Lonnie had wanted to bring a friend along to help tackle the 600-pound calf, but couldn't find anyone at the last minute. He guessed he and my uncle would wrestle her down alone and told my uncle he hoped to be able to rope her the first time, because it would be easier. My uncle laughed.

"We weren't going to have a second chance," he says.

Because of the brush situation, Lonnie had to approach the calf on foot and warily eyed her red coat peeking through the cedars. She hadn't eaten any of the feed and appeared unwilling to cooperate.

Then suddenly, she stepped out of the trees. Just like that. Presented herself to Lonnie and my uncle to be roped. So Lonnie coiled up his rope, circled the air a few times with it, settled it down neatly over Lucy's head and foreleg, and it was done. Just like that.

One thing Lonnie had noticed right off was that Lucy wasn't a 600-pound cow. Maybe half that. Maybe. Probably not even half. So when he and my uncle landed her on the ground, they didn't have much of a problem. Lucy complied with the same indifferent agreeability she had shown through much of her escapade.

"Through all this," says my uncle, "she was never wild. She wasn't a real wild calf. She was fairly tame to a point, but she wouldn't let you get real close to her."

But my uncle decided he'd had enough of the search-and-retrieve routine, and he returned her to the rancher, who amicably handed back the neat pile of bills and said he wasn't surprised. "Brahmas are jumpers, he said. They're standoffish with other cows and clannish with their own kind. Look for one Brahma on your ranch, and you've found them all."

"Sure enough," says my uncle. Looking out over that Blanco ranch, he could see the Brahmas. They were standing off in a clump by themselves over near the fence.

And with them was Lucy, polite dreamer with springs in her legs and a passion for unfenced fields, for the airborne music of flight.

She's young still. She may have a goal. Passion feeds dreams. Who says the cow can't jump over the moon?

Beginning of School

The beginning of school comes with both regret and relief for most parents, and for many children.

The regret mourns the passage of a leisure time, a time when rules relax a little, curfews extend, wake-up calls come later, if at all. Regret sees the hours in the river slip away, sees the tightening of schedules, the making of lunches at daybreak, the hustling of half-awake children. It takes on homework, school clothes, PTO, Show and Tell.

Relief is the other side of the coin — knowing where your children will be going five days a week while you are at work, knowing that they will be entertained with something other than Nickelodeon, knowing that they might actually learn something.

My children are excited about the start of school. The oldest, Malone, is in second grade and enters learning as a competitive sport. His small steel trap of a mind compartmentalizes things, sorts them, stores them, categorizes. In short, he is an organizer. Where he came by that trait is something I wonder about occasionally. He didn't get it from me.

School supplies fascinate him. He takes on the Back to School aisle as a welcome challenge. I take it on as an unwelcome challenge, at best. When school supplies hit the shelves in

July (the way Christmas gewgaws hit the shelves in August), we argue about how soon we need to buy pencils. I am leery of buying them too soon, for fear they will disappear in the ensuing weeks. He is leery of buying them too late, for fear they will simply disappear off the shelves before he has a chance to choose the ones he wants.

Also, he has pointed out with a child's convoluted logic that if I buy them for him in July and he loses them, I will still have time to buy him more before school starts.

I try to remember how it felt to have more pencils and paper than I knew I could use, the satisfied feeling of knowing that I would not run out, that abundance would follow me through the year, that I could write and write and write, and when my pencil lead neared my eraser, I could simply reach for another pencil, and it was always there—bright yellow and begging to be sharpened.

Reams of paper inspired me. I could fill the sheets with words and make mistakes, and there would be more clean sheets to right the wrongs.

Notebooks always suggested to me the possibility of organization. They had dividers that might order the world, make life easier, given half a chance. I never gave them even that and have finally come to accept that I function better in chaos than order, but the idea appealed to me. Still does, sometimes.

So I try to be more understanding of the driving need for school supplies, although I do not buy them in July, for purely economic reasons: I don't want to have to buy them again in August.

And once we've bought them, I know how my son will spend the afternoon. He will devote hours to figuring the best way to organize the pencils and the crayons and the markers and the folders and the notebooks. He will make them all fit in the new backpack, with no wasted space, and then he will show me how he did it by taking it all out again and starting over.

I stop and watch him during the process with a painful love. I wish I could guarantee the order in his world with the kind of faith he has in his school supplies, but I know that sometimes when you take the pieces out of your backpack to show the people you love how you have ordered your life, they don't always fit back the same way you had them the first time. They should, but sometimes they don't. And you stand over the full backpack with the box of crayons in your hands, trying to figure out why they fit in earlier, and they won't fit now.

I attribute it to the devious order that drives chaos, but I don't tell him that. Maybe he'll be better at packing a backpack than I am.

He looks forward to school because he's beginning to learn about learning. He reads words that amaze me. When he sailed right through "Connecticut" the other day without even pausing, I expressed surprise—and delight.

He looked at me patronizingly and said, "Mother, I know that word from Monopoly."

Oh.

When he conquered another word that was not in the Monopoly game, and I once again praised him, he explained patiently that he was taking phonics. I explained to him that it had been a long time since I learned to read, and I'm impressed that anyone can master the concepts. He shook his head and read on.

He's eager, impatient with lulls in the day, insistent on obeying the letter of the teacher's law. I try to honor that, catching myself when I start to bend the rules to fit my schedule, more an adherent to the spirit of the law than the letter. I remind myself that breaking the rules works only after you've learned the discipline of following them, only after you've learned the reason for the rules in the first place.

Cameron attends Pre-K at St. Stephen's and looked forward to school with unmitigated enthusiasm from the moment I told him I would buy him light-up shoes and a backpack. That's all it took. I wish I could make everyone that happy.

Cameron's not concerned with packing his backpack. It doesn't matter that he has nothing to put in it. Simply wearing it is enough. He stuffs it with his lunch box, and if that contains an egg salad sandwich, he's happy. Order, to him, is whatever lies in front of him at the moment.

My challenge with Cameron is Show and Tell. Last year, his teacher called it Science and told the parents the children could bring whatever they wanted to bring. She would somehow turn it into Science.

So Cameron brought his firetruck. Again and again and again. I know that patient, kind, loving lady cringed inside when she saw Cameron drive that firetruck through the Pre-K door time and again. How much can you find to say about a small plastic firetruck with an insistent siren? But she never said a word and always expressed delight and surprise when the firetruck took its place on the Science stand.

This year, his teacher has asked the children not to bring toys, but to bring objects that have more educational value, and Cameron is at a loss. For one thing, he left the firetruck out in the rain, the batteries shorted, and the siren began an unending wail. When I disconnected the batteries, it seems I also disconnected some of the lure of the firetruck, and it has been out of commission since then.

But he comes up with ideas. Often, they're last-minute. On weekday mornings, as I'm herding him and his brother into the car, he'll make a break and run back into the house to find the conch shell I brought back from the Caribbean fourteen years ago. Or he'll fight almost to the death with Malone over the drying shell of a cicada.

Earlier this week, after searching the neighborhood for him so I could take him to school, I found him crouched in a neighbor's driveway, intently scrutinizing the earth. I called impatiently, but he stayed glued to the driveway. Finally, I backed the car out and honked my horn, which caught his attention.

He leaped onto his small red bicycle and came careening down the street toward the house, his training wheels humming in the morning air, never coming close to the pavement. His older brother watched in disgust and muttered something about babies and training wheels and why did Cameron have to keep them on his bike when he didn't need them anymore.

I reminded Malone that once, a long time ago, he had been four and had training wheels on his bike. He ignored me, the memory too painful to recall.

When Cameron climbed in the car, he had, clutched in his triumphant sweaty hand, his Show and Tell—a lizard's tail. How, I asked, had he found only the *tail* of a lizard, and a small lizard, at that?

Well, he said, he had been trying to catch the lizard when I called and then honked. Realizing he was running out of time, he was less than delicate and somehow pulled the tail off the lizard. But it was okay, he said. The tail would grow back, and now he had a lizard tail to show his class.

The tail was about two inches long and brown. I know that because somehow, on the way to school, he lost it, and I had to help find it. I had to dig through the debris of the back seat, a distant country occupied solely by small children, until we found the pointy little brown thing, but we did find it, which sustains my theory that somewhere in the midst of chaos, order does exist, although some people probably call it luck.

Later in the week, a fast-breaking news call turned up the fact that iridescent green, beetle-like creatures were swarming around a large oak tree outside Cavalry Graphics. Would I please come down and take a picture? Upon arriving at the scene, I discovered hundreds of the insects winging through the air. The friend who had called said that earlier that day, she had seen millions at the base of the oak tree, a whole shimmering mass of green and gold. The owner of Cavalry Graphics suggested that perhaps we were witnessing an alien invasion.

My friend scooped a few of the winged creatures into a jar and gave them to me to identify. Turns out they're green June beetles, which seems appropriate enough, and I gave them to Cameron for Show and Tell. By then, of course, the beetles were waning, though still alive, and smelled very bad. That made them even more attractive.

Cameron was thrilled. He and Malone would smell the bottle, push it away at arm's length with screwed-up faces, then pull it back, smell it again.

School is good, he's decided. At four years old, if you have a backpack stuffed with an egg salad sandwich, light-up shoes on your feet, and your Show and Tell in hand, there's order in the world.

We're ready for it. Give us nine months, and we'll be searching out chaos. Thank God for balance. Life goes on.

 Redbird

It's a winter scene: through the windows, graduating grays, the river breathing steam, the stark branches of the yaupon tapping against the glass.

Gray limestone, grayer clouds, gone to pewter in the February sky. Outside, a chill that harbors rain or morning fog, that muffles the distance so the world seems close and silver and silent.

What breaks the gray are the holly berries, scarlet drops along the bare yaupon. Christmas gone, the ritual of green and red and candlelight stored in the past, and all muted now, gone dormant, slipped under the gray to breathe an even sleep.

Except for the redbird. He must sense something we don't know — an impending season, an edge to the gray that will soften into blues and greens and sunflowers.

In this world of hush and understatement, he is a rage of springtime and hormones. He sees a future and a possibility, and he hurls himself against the cold glass in some seasonal passion abated only by nighttime and the blessed closure of dark.

Springtime is no gentle awakening for this fellow. He has fought out the winter, lent his startling scarlet to the gray and the companionship of yaupon berries. He has waited, lived alongside some longing until he felt something turn inside and signal the season.

And the people who bought the house six months ago, who

have moved into it now with dreams of peace and retirement, rise in the first striving sunlight to the steady thud of a small, red-feathered body hurling itself against the windows in some frenzied celebration of spring.

At first, they thought the cardinal was crazed, demented, bent on self-destruction. He'll hurt himself, they worried. He'll knock himself out.

And they were puzzled. He threw himself at all the windows of the house indiscriminately, seeming to prefer the windows nearest them, hell-bent on something or other. Maybe, they reasoned, he was trying to get inside, which wasn't an option. Or maybe he could be appeased.

So the man hied himself up to the feed store, one of his favorite haunts anyway. He'd bought a pair of roughout, pointy-toed cowboy boots there years ago, when they carried boots, and still remembers them fondly. And he likes to browse through the tools, dreaming about what he could do with them if he had the time and knew how to use them.

But this time he was looking for sunflower seeds, because cardinals have a thing for sunflower seeds, and he was looking for anything that might appease the appetite that that drove the red body against his windows.

So, armed with enough seed for a redbird banquet, he scattered it far from the windows and in containers on the deck to lure the bird away from the glass.

To no avail. Perhaps the seeds renewed the bird's energy. From dawn 'til dusk, he beat his unsteady rhythm against the windows, his protest against the unbroken grays around him. He woke the people each morning, shattered reveries of peace, interrupted phone calls, battered the glass 'til it was streaked with the efforts of his anger.

And then another unsteady rhythm broke the peace, and the woman's heart pumped an uneven load of blood through her body, lodging it momentarily in the brain and confusing her world past the grays and the fluttering reds that had been her welcome to her new home.

Now it was the hospital, and when the fear cleared, and her

blood thinned, and her wild heart calmed, she turned her thoughts back to the redbird. Her daughter called from the house, and she could hear it beating itself against the glass.

"We have to do something," she said. "We can't go home to this."

The man suggested netting the house, then swooping the net around the bird in one fell gesture. Or perhaps standing at the window and blasting through it at the bird with a shotgun. Or employing the services of his six-year-old grandson to help him devise a plan.

The woman eyed him warily. She had not lost her sense of humor and hoped he had not lost his. Perhaps, it was suggested, he should call the Audubon Society.

Between the two of them, they were gentle enough people. They didn't want to harm the bird, but it was unnerving. They hadn't moved there to be the dive-bomb target of a cardinal.

"You can laugh," the woman said, "but try living with those sudden red explosions. They catch you by surprise."

So the man called the Audubon Society, reached a recording, and learned a few things. He learned that if you drive out into the country a couple of miles, take a right past the red gate beside the Spanish oak, maneuver the pot holes for a third of a mile, hang a left at the caliche road marked by a torch-cut metal roadrunner, drive another quarter-mile, park, and survey the cedar brake for a while, you might catch a glimpse of the orange-crested oak dancer.

Or if you drive out in the country in the opposite direction, turn left at the gap near the third fence post ...

Or you could leave a message. So he left a message, something about a crazy cardinal. Could they help?

Then he called the Parks and Wildlife people and learned something else. The bird was not crazy, they said. It was a perfectly normal male cardinal vesting himself in the rites of spring. February had turned its corner, they said, and while the world still hunkered in some silver sleep, the cardinal felt his red blood rise and cry out for a lady love, a nest, a yard to call his own.

He was protecting his territory, striking out at would-be

suitors to his dream. He was jealous of all red feathers in the trees and would fly against his contenders at any cost to protect that dream. He would secure his area until the right mate alighted on his cedar limb, and he would continue that jealous frenzy until the eggs were laid and the fledglings hatched and gone. He would forego sunflower seeds and rainwater for his hormonal rage.

The man thought on that for a while. Hormones, he reflected. They strike us all. Might have been a time, he remembered, when hormones drove the springtime through him like some red-feathered frenzy. When the lady lying in the bed was looking for a cedar branch on which to build a nest. When children stumbled from that nest and took their turns falling through the air before their wings could learn to catch it.

Might have been a time when he battered his heart in defense of a dream, of territory. Might be, he thought, looking at the lady in the hospital bed, the heart still batters itself to protect what it loves.

Later, the Audubon Society called. The bird was not crazy, they said. It was a perfectly normal male cardinal. Its hormones ...

The man gave it some more thought. The next morning, he stood on the bench on his deck, eye level with the hot-blooded bird, and stared back into his house. With the sunlight glancing off the windows, he could see shining back at him a reflection of gray limbs, gray limestone, red yaupon berries, and his own bemused face.

He returned to the hospital that day to tell his wife he saw himself in the window. The bird, he says, is fighting himself. He's protecting his world from his own reflection, an interesting concept. At times, not a bad one.

They thought on it for a while. They could cover all the windows in newspaper. They could hang noisemakers from the eaves of the house or tape pictures of predators—hawks, owls, cats—to their view of the river.

The lady sat straighter in the bed. She was coming home any day now, and they would find a solution that would not involve shotguns through the windows or a house papered in yesterday's news. The weather forecaster was promising clearing skies and the whistle of March winds. A new life was in the making out there, and there was too much to do to lie abed in fear.

New seasons bring new colors, and spring can bring ease, as well as abandon. Some rhythms we must learn to live with, pay attention to their syncopations, be grateful for the life that spurs them.

She's home now, measuring the floor space for her furniture, the days for her future.

And the cardinal is flying against the windows. He won't learn to recognize himself in attack. But the man and the woman are looking for solutions, a way to soften or deflect the uneven rhythms, a way to share their space with the season.

Rain

"Linda! Come quick! Look at this! Now! Before you miss it!"

I stumbled from my desk and through the maze of partitions that form this modern-day office, out of the fluorescent light toward the windows, where a gray light broke the sky like morning. Only it was late afternoon, and the light was filtering through the rain, through the great, fat drops of rain, the water falling through the air like an end to abstinence, like the birth of waterfalls or lakes or oceans. Rain.

It's been too long and too dry since the last drink of water. The world has shriveled and grown petty in its shriveling. Small grievances annoy like catastrophes, and catastrophes march the dusty road of the commonplace when there is no water for the tears. It's been too long, too hot, too dry.

So I stood at the window with everyone else in the office and watched the gutters spout their philosophy of excess, watched the water unbraid furiously from the roof to the pavement, Rapunzel's long hair turned liquid and loose.

Oh, it was a fine storm, a storm to dance in if one were so inclined, and as we stared out the window toward the street, focusing on falling water, we saw a man dance out across the road with something like a broom in his hands and begin to waltz in the rain.

"What's he doing?" someone asked.

"Getting wet," someone offered.

"Cleaning the street? Sweeping the water?"

"He's dancing," I said. "He's dancing in the rain."

Probably, though, he wasn't. As he bent down to sweep something into a box, we decided he'd dropped a bunch of nails in the road and figured this was as good a time as any to clean them up. And it was. You can still get flat tires in the rain.

But I wanted to believe he was dancing. In times of drought, the world becomes too literal, too grounded, and when the world is too dry, what lifts from the ground is dust and the crazed hot air of desperation.

I wanted to dance in the rain. I wanted to drink it and slide in it and fall with it. I wanted it to go on forever, an endless music—percussion and wind. I wanted to dance in it.

But my work clothes stopped me, and the world was too much with me, and the closest I came was to brave the front porch so I could smell the wetness and feel the cool air that was not August in Texas, but part of some long-running dream of relief. I was a little disappointed in myself, but I err always on the grim side of safety.

I have a friend who dances in rain. When the torrents hit, he was in the lumberyard parking lot, counting planks of wood with his sister. This man has a big, brave voice that won't stop singing, and he has been singing a rain song at least half the summer. When the rain hit, it was answer to song, which is prayer to many, and celebration when the notes hit their mark.

So he danced in the parking lot while everyone else stood back, like me, under the eaves of the porch and watched. He turned his face into the rain and let it fall around him with the full permission we grant the force of nature. When the rain stopped—and it was brief—he shook the water from him like some great bear and walked inside. He said he thought people might avoid him and speak in whispers around him, but he was wrong. People crowded him, as close to the dancer as they could let themselves be, as close to the joy of the rain.

It's all right that we don't all dance in the rain. Rain is why God invented porches, rain and the sun that follows. And without porches, what would go on the front end of houses? Without porches, what would shade the rest of us from that slippery dance and let us appreciate the performance, celebrate from a distance the wild, wet wonder of the rain?

So I stood on the porch outside my office and breathed it. It carried the odors of my childhood, of wet cedar and caliche puddles, the faint sulfur of lightning. It carried the memory of one late, dry August when a rain had broken the monotonous spell of heat and we watched it slant through the porch screens of the weathered summer house we called our home. When it finally drew back in wisps of steam from the August earth, we ventured outside to the driveway, which turned to a cloudy pool of caliche water.

My brothers and I stood back in the grass under the dripping cedars, looking at the familiar world as if we expected to find it changed. And it had. My mother had been growing crosser as the heat increased, and her five children milled through it like angry gnats. Irritations had surfaced and swarmed like insects or cactus spines, invisible and embedded in the skin.

But that one wild rain had changed all that. My mother's back relaxed. Her shoulders dropped. Her hands released the grip they had taken on her upper arms, crossed in an effort at control. And she began to dance.

(A rain dance has no measured steps. You cannot memorize its beat. And if you choose a partner, you must be willing both to step on toes and twirl through mud. A rain dance knows no etiquette.)

My mother's arms lifted from her side, and she became younger than we were. She danced into that driveway, past the rain-streaked cars, into the mud, and she squished it between her toes and laughed until we could not resist becoming her partners. The tensions of late summer, of heat and boredom, fell away with the sheets of the rain that had broken across these hills like gray silk scarves in the afternoon wind. Suddenly, the world opened itself to possibility, and all that had been limp with the dryness of despair broke loose and lifted its head and bloomed in an overnight greening.

So I guess I have danced in rain. I was younger then, and no one knew my name. I didn't care if they did. I fell prey to hope and promise, and the rain only fed it, egged it on. I won't deny the dry spells, but all it takes is a little falling water, a little bit of rain.

I know that Wednesday's rain probably didn't signal the end of anything, but this morning, I woke to the sound of water in a thirsty creek. I woke to cooler air, and a coverlet pulled across the sheet, to black branches shaded in greener leaves. I woke to the leavings of the rain.

Rain. It feels so good to say the word. If I were of a mind to have another child, I think I would name the child that word of promise. I think I would name the child Rain.

Pet Parade

Sometimes life gets in the way of what you're supposed to be doing. Last week, I had schedules that ran a parallel track— one career-oriented, the other child-oriented. While my heart lay with my child, I had scheduled the job first, and so I missed the Pet Parade.

The Pet Parade is an annual event that occurs during "P" week at Scudder Primary School, usually following Pajama Day. Participants include kindergarteners, their pets, and, often as not, their parents. While I knew I couldn't attend the parade, I could at least help my kindergartener get ready for it. That entailed several things, the first one being to remember the parade far enough in advance to get the dog a haircut, and that's not as easy as it sounds.

Wimberley is a town full of dogs, and most of the ones I know don't go in for haircuts, but there must be plenty that do because the groomer is always booked weeks in advance. With two jobs and two children, I believe in the order and logic of chaos and try not to plan my personal life too far in advance, for fear I will forget it.

So the dog has meandered through the summer with his silky white feathers matted in cockleburs and dried grasses. He's a swimmer, an animal who moves more gracefully through water than he does on land. On land, he ambles and shags and drags his big frame through the heat with the long-suffering patience of an ancient breed—the mutt. In the water, he floats with the grace of a downwind leaf. He is weightless and cool, and he never dries out all summer long.

His name is Bob, and he is the most patient of animals, a gift of a dog who has carried me through ten and a half years with an unrelenting calm that breaks only when he sees a cat or another dog in the back of a pickup truck. He himself won't ride in the back of a truck but opts for the inside of a car—a seat if it's available. He thinks I'm his mother and breaks into high-pitched yaps when I drive up. He won't eat when I'm gone, and he's been known to sit in the middle of the road and howl until I came home. He loves me.

He's big—a cross between an ambitious springer spaniel and an accommodating Newfoundland. At 100 pounds, he acts like a cream puff and smells like rank creek water. I don't really care. I love the big goof, but I am sensitive to the sensitivities of others, and I didn't think I could inflict Bob's signature odor on the Pet Parade and its viewers, so I finagled an appointment with his hairdresser.

I was lucky. I managed to get him in the day before the parade, but only, I think, because the groomer has three broken toes and wasn't taking many clients, particularly big ones. I must have sounded desperate, though, and one of the other veterinary assistants offered to try to groom Bob if I wasn't concerned about a "show dog" haircut. I assured her I wasn't.

When I called the vet to check on Bob, the assistant informed me that the groomer with the broken toes had taken pity on her and sat on the floor, her leg stretched out in front of her in a red cast, and helped cut the matted cockleburs from Bob's black-and-white coat. Some of them, she said, were embedded pretty deep, and only Bob would have stood for the hours of grooming necessary to remove them.

But they did an impressive job. The dog that met me at the door to the clinic with high, bright yaps looked like a puppy, shorn and soft and sweet-smelling. He was parade-ready, as they say in the business.

That left only the parade to be accomplished. The morning of the parade, I woke the children early, poured cereal, pointed

out toothbrushes and shoes, divvied up lunch money, and hunted frantically for a leash.

Bob is unaccustomed to leashes and goes very unwillingly or not at all when attached to one unless I am at the other end of it, and then he doesn't really need one. So leashes are scarce at my house. As I pulled open drawers, I remembered seeing one tied high up in a cedar with a rock swinging from the loose end. It was a fleeting image, but clear enough for me to acknowledge that I wasn't going to climb to the top of the cedar to retrieve it.

So I unearthed the one he'd worn home with his new haircut, loaded my children and my dog into a friend's van, and waved goodbye as they drove away, with Bob peering after me from the window of the van, nonplussed.

Since my mother wanted to see the parade, I went back into the house to call her and tell her the parade participants were on their way.

From here on out, it's all hearsay, secondhand, as it were, embellished truths. But that is what history is made of — memory and perception and the singular details of personal experience. Although I did not attend this parade, it stands in my mind as one of the most memorable parades I have never seen.

First you must picture Cameron, my son. At five, he is all red curls and dark eyes, with a fine dusting of freckles across the bridge of his nose. He weighs half of what Bob weighs and is given to sucking his thumb, to belly-deep laughter, to cartwheels, and a fierce flash of pride that incorporates the thumb in the mouth and a sudden turning away. Coaxing won't turn him back or heal the wounded pride. Only time interrupts that concentration.

He loves the dog. He crawls across Bob's broad back and tries to ride him. Bob solves the problem by sitting down. He comforts himself when he is tired by using Bob's matted side as a pillow. Bob accommodates by stretching his heavy frame a little longer and sighing the sigh of the infinitely patient.

I think Cameron was proud to accompany Bob in the parade. In the past, he has owned hamsters and goldfish and lizards, but none have matched Bob in endurance or inertia. He has outlived them all.

Now, as I understand it, the participants in the Pet Parade

were many and diverse. There were cats and dogs and goats and goldfish and rabbits and lots and lots of children. They were divided up as classes, each class parading through the parking lot separately with its animals, the parents standing in the background, smiling, ready to jump in at any moment to break up any hint of antagonism on the part of the parade participants.

For the most part, there were no disturbances. My mother tells me that Bob, up until the end, was probably one of the best behaved of the parade participants. She was concerned about the rabbits, as she had heard that rabbits, with their history of timidity, can even keel over dead from fright if frightened enough.

Those rabbits, said my mother, were in a cage right in front of a dog, and the dog was more than a little interested in the rabbits. He had his nose up against the cage, and she was sure those rabbits were heart-attack candidates. But my friend said he heard the parent that belonged to the child with the rabbit saying those rabbits were laughing at that dog. Those rabbits, said the parent, own their own dogs, and they know what to do with them. Laugh. Dogs can't get in a rabbit cage.

So, complete with laughing rabbits, the parade wended its way through the parking lot, and all went well until Bob decided he'd paraded about all he was going to parade and stopped.

I once saw a t-shirt on a guy selling firecrackers. Both the t-shirt and the firecracker salesman were a little worse for wear, but as my sons lingered over each bright package in the booth, I had time to make out the message on the t-shirt. It showed a big mountain of a dog, shaggy, black-and-white—not unlike Bob—and a very small man scaling the dog's side. It said, "You can move a mountain, but you can't budge a big dog."

I think that's true. According to Cameron, he tried. He pulled on the blue nylon rope, and Bob sat down. Then, said Cameron, he lay down.

My friend described it well. "The best part of the parade thing," he said, "was when Bob decided he wasn't going anywhere. Three-quarters of the way around the parade circle he said *No mas* and lay down."

I believe that Bob and I share something in common. As I

grow older, I am convinced that under my layers of socialization and civilization, I am at heart a passive anarchist. As I grow older, I balk at unreason and paperwork. Sometimes, I find myself lying down in the midst of it, refusing to move, not unlike Bob's resistance to the Pet Parade, his unwillingness to take things to an unreasonable extreme.

Everyone tried to help, but Bob was done with the parade. Teachers tried to help. My mother tried to help. But Bob was through. As I had pointed out to the veterinary assistant, Bob was no show dog, and he had no intention of starting up now. *No mas,* he said and lay down.

Cameron gave it all he had. He entreated, he cajoled, but mostly he pulled. The problem, he said, was that Bob's collar kept slipping over his head because he'd had a haircut and was not as big as he used to be. At any rate, Bob lay there, a black-and-white blob of passive resistance, until another dog decided to help and nosed his way into the situation.

That got Bob's attention. He sat up and said "Harumph!" to the other dog, then lay back down again. No doubt about it, he was holding the parade up in a noticeable way, so Cameron, grounded at moments in the practical world, opted for brute strength.

"Jimmeeee!" he shouted, entreating my friend, who is much taller than Bob and easily twice his weight, to fix the problem.

Jimmy had been taking pictures but abandoned the camera long enough to encourage Bob to finish the parade. When I asked Cameron how he did it, he said Jimmy grabbed Bob by the collar and lifted him to his feet. I can see it now. Unwilling to move, Bob probably had his legs stiff and his body plied backward at a 45-degree angle so that he skidded across the pavement as Jimmy dragged him the ten feet to the curb and the end of the parade.

Jimmy's version is gentler. He says he convinced him. He outweighed him, and Bob eventually gave in to reason.

(Bob, by the way, was not the only anarchist. The goat was also opposed to authority and gave a pretty good rendition of intractability, but he weighed less than Bob and was more easily persuaded.)

Then, says Cameron, when they reached the curb, Bob sat

down on his foot. He didn't mind that, he says. It actually felt kind of good, but he didn't like it when Bob lay down on his feet because it made it hard to move and Bob was getting heavier. Finally, they both called a truce—Cameron sat down on the curb next to a friend with a stuffed animal and stuck his thumb in his mouth. Bob stretched out on the sidewalk beside him, full length, and gave way to oblivion, ignoring the rest of the parade.

And then it was over. Some of the better-behaved and smaller animals were allowed to stay—the goldfish and possibly the rabbits—but Bob was taken home, where he promptly made a desultory pass at the cat who lives in the garage, dug a deeper hole beneath the mountain laurel bush, turned around twice, lay down, and drifted back into oblivion or anarchy or wherever his dreams led him through the cool, dappled green of the mountain laurel leaves.

The parade was over. He was glad to be home.

# Smokey the Pony

I remember a little black pony, part Welsh, part Shetland, sleek round belly bending the tall grasses, short, stocky legs strutting out the steps that kept him one nose ahead of the big horses, his velvety lips drawn back in an actual smile.

His name was Smokey, and he died last month, having lived longer than any pony I've ever heard of, longer than ponies are supposed to live. Smokey was forty when he died, and the families he made himself a part of — the Williams, the Gumberts, the Johnsons — threw him a wake, of sorts.

Technically, a wake is held in the presence of the departed's body, but since Smokey had died and been interred several days earlier with the help of a backhoe, the wake was held in the absence of his body — so perhaps it was more of a memorial service.

Like most big families, the families who loved Smokey have scattered themselves across the country, but those who could not make the wake either mailed or faxed their memories. Among them were my brothers, my sister, and my cousin, the children who had ridden Smokey with such pride through the meadows high in firewheel and wild coreopsis, through the lights of the rodeo arenas, the pastures punctuated with racing poles.

Smokey was a pole racer. He didn't have it in him to take life in a leisurely fashion. He was a performer, a rodeo star. He pulled carriages through parades and at international carriage meets. He carried generations of children through the hills and ravines and meadows and back roads, always at the front of the herd.

For me, and for my family, he was part of summertime. My parents bought him from Marsha Johnson in the early 1970s for the younger children to ride. By the time Smokey moved inside our fence, my legs, which are none too long to begin with, could almost touch the ground when I sat on Smokey's back, so I opted for the bigger horses. But for my younger brothers, and then my sister, he was the perfect size.

Marsha had bought Smokey from Lee Rodgers, whose parents had bought him from Mr. Lackey in San Marcos in 1961 when Smokey was five years old. Lee immediately recognized Smokey's worth. In a memoir written from Germany after Smokey's death, Lee recalls, "Pound per pound, Smokey was one of the best horses I ever owned. Smokey was easy to haul around. He would jump in the back of a pickup just like your good Texas cowdog. He didn't need any sideboards to support him. Who needed an expensive horse trailer with Smokey?"

Lee used Smokey to pull his buggy through Market Day and Halloween parades, won blue ribbons in the 4-H Playday Key Hole races astride Smokey's low back, and hunted rabbit and armadillo from a better vantage point than most horsemen.

My younger brothers rode Smokey in the Wimberley 4-H Playdays for years. Coming from California to summer in Wimberley, they wore a different style than most of the young cowboys that breathed the dust of the rodeo arena, but they could ride that low-slung pony just as well.

One of my most vivid memories is of my oldest younger brother, Bob, hatless, dressed in neon tank top, shorts, and tennis shoes, waiting at the gate for his turn to take the poles. As he reined in Smoke's inveterate impatience, we heard the announcer, with his long Texas drawl that could turn *bug* into a two-syllable word, say, "And our next contestant will be Bob Williams on Squatlow!"

He brought the stands down in laughter when the miniature steed exploded through the gates, legs whirling like windmill

blades, his lips drawn back in the smile that competition always brought to his lips.

On one Playday, Bob and my youngest brother, David, decided they would capitalize on Smokey's lack of stature and participate in the Rescue Race, which involves a rider on horseback scooping up his partner from the rodeo floor, dumping him on the back of the horse, and racing back to the finish line.

As Bob puts it in the memoir he sent to Smokey's wake, "David and I once took advantage of Smokey's architecture in the Rescue Race at one of the 4-H Playdays. Unfortunately, we fell prey to another aspect of his architecture, which made it difficult sometimes to securely cinch a saddle. The two of us became human saddlebags after the saddle blanket with the stirrups made its way under Smokey's ample belly. We counterbalanced each other and counted hoof beats as we slipped closer to the ground."

My father's memory of the event takes poetic form, as follows:

"Squatlow was an a.k.a.,
  his registered name was Smokey.
He never acknowledged the announcer's humor,
  we all thought it was hokey.
Now Smokey knew the barrel trick,
  he had always won hands down,
  the problem was the saddle girth
  that began to come unwound.
At sonic speeds so close to earth
  great energies transition,
  before the finish line was reached, saddle, girth,
  rider changed position.
The judges checked, rule book words
  said clearly horse and rider,
  and no interpretation, right or wrong,
  could be made for horse and slider.
But Smokey knew he'd won that race.
Bob's problem was the girth.
He had failed to compensate for physics
  of sonic travel close to earth."

Smokey charged through life with the same fervor that impelled him through the rodeo gates. The pony didn't know how to walk. Some said it was because his legs were short, but I hold that was only logic's excuse. Smokey ran all the time because he wanted to be first, because his heart beat out a rhythm that his feet danced to, because he didn't want to be late to the party or last to the feedbag. He ran because he loved the feel of the wind against his teeth (remember, he was smiling), because it felt good, because he loved to run.

And if you happened to be the one riding him, you endured the sideache, complicated by the laughter, for the sheer pleasure of passing all the big guys and bumping along through the knee-high flowers in front of them all. You had to let people know you were coming, though, had to call out, "Smokey on your right!" or you faced the possibility of collision. People riding him for the first time were known to sweep past the other horses, crying, "How do I stop this guy?"

Gradually, as happens to most of us, Smokey grew older. At first you couldn't tell by looking at him. Rotund until the last few years, he ate more than his weight in feed. He grayed around the temples a bit, but some said it gave him more credibility, an air of distinction.

As he aged, in deference to his years (which he never seemed to notice), the children who had grown up on his back, and who now had legs that would drag the ground, gave up riding him. He became the official transporter of small children, whom he loved.

Mostly, he hung out at the Gumberts' house. Given free range of the ranch, he chose to be near people, or the other horses when he could find them. If he wasn't standing in the driveway, you could probably find him standing near the fenced pasture where the bigger horses lived. They were good friends.

Sometimes, when the Gumberts weren't around, he wandered down the road to the weekend rent cabins, where children played in the yard and along the creek. The Gumberts returned more than once to find him meandering back to the house, his mane and tail braided in wildflowers, or feathers from the chickens, guineas, and turkeys that scratched their living out of the soil near the rent cabins.

He loved to eat, and, as the Gumberts take as many of their meals outside as possible, he would join them on the patio, his taste for food growing more diverse with his years. Particularly, says Eddie, he seemed to enjoy fresh fruits, vegetables, and pastas, but, like many vegetarians, given the proper circumstances, he would even eat meat.

It was not at all unusual to visit the Gumberts in the mornings, the patio leafy with wisteria and grapevine, Cypress Creek flowing both shallow and deep below Park's Peak, and find Smokey shouldered up against the picnic table, munching on toast and mustang grape jelly.

My youngest brother, David, said, "As I grew older and taller, Smokey seemed more like a pet than a horse. Waking up in the morning and having breakfast on the patio seemed fitting for an old friend."

In his last years, Smokey developed cancer. His trot finally slowed to a walk, and for several winters everyone predicted his demise. With the progression of the cancer, he began to lose weight, but it didn't seem to faze him. He never lost interest in food or good company, a bon vivant to the end.

The end came quietly. No drama. Smokey lay down one night and died. We all knew it was coming, had watched him for months, the black coat melting into the gray, which seemed to dissipate a little each day, a gradual fade, as if he might simply vaporize into the early-summer air and be gone, a dream of a good small horse.

But it didn't happen that way. Dorothy Gumbert found him early one morning lying near the horse pasture where he had been visiting with his bigger friends, a small, bony body that gave out after forty years. It was a sunny weekend, bordering on summer heat, and as the sun climbed the edges of the wispy clouds, we searched harder and harder for a backhoe. Bill Johnson came through for the small horse, whose grave marker he had already carved from a slab of native walnut and painted.

The wake was not a sad one. People laughed a lot and ate pasta in Smokey's memory. For almost two solid hours, they told Smokey stories, focused on the big spirit in the small body, said goodbye to a friend.

He's out there somewhere. He's smiling and trotting, and wildflowers tickle his round belly. When he stops, small fingers plait his mane with bluebonnets, with winecups, with the bright silver feathers that drift from the wings of the angels.

Bedtime

The bed is getting crowded now when I lie down at night to read to my sons. They used to lie, one on either side, tucked into my arms, which held the book hanging above us until my arms grew tired. That way, we could all see the pictures.

Now I sit at one end, and they sprawl across the sheets, but they still listen. We finished *Dr. Doolittle* the other night, and we've embarked on *The Just So Stories.* I'm waiting to get my hands on *The Swiss Family Robinson.*

It's a tradition I remember from my childhood, one that may have shaped my outlook on the world more than many of the traditions my parents sought to pass on to their five children. I grew up in a world of princesses and chivalry, of secret gardens and magic cats. I toured Middle Earth with the hobbit and cried when the mermaid left her cold, silver water for a wordless love. The ice queen chilled my bones, and I tumbled through the rhythms of classic poetry on my way to sleep.

I grew up with a passion for language, a belief in the pure beauty of the word. Plots were nice. Plots were important, but without the rich trappings of the words that built them, they were spare skeletons on the page, devoid of color, road maps in black and white.

Words, chosen carefully, were the deep plum velvet of nightfall down those leafy roads. They were the angel plumage of swans, the golden swells of Rapunzel's loosened hair.

It was the words that lined my dreams with satin and the coarse rug-burn weave of brown burlap. It was the words that gave texture to the world.

So I lie down with my children many nights and talk them through the old stories. I feel kind of guilty sometimes, as if I am neglecting the contemporary, opting for dead writers over those still spinning the words. But I figure if no one reads the older tales, they, like Tinkerbell, will fade. Time is left for the newer ones, and I guess I love the comfort of familiarity. These are elegant old friends.

When Malone was younger, I held him in my lap in the green chintz rocker and read him *The Tale of Jeremy Fisher* until he could recite the whole page, and often did if I paused too long in my reading. He was two or three, barely old enough to carry on connected conversations, but he had Beatrix Potter down. He knew about frogs and lily pads.

He also knew if, in an effort to condense, I tried to skip a paragraph or a page of one of his favorite books. Politely, he would point out that I seemed to have missed part of the story, and then he would recite to me what I had left out.

Later, he wanted me to read him *Anno's Counting Book,* a sad turn of events for me because I never considered mathematics inspirational. He does, though, and I'm glad of it. I wonder if it had to do with the counting book.

Cameron wanted only train books for a while, and when I balked at *The Little Engine That Could* for the third night in a row, he would concede to *Mr. Milligan's Steam Shovel.*

Sometimes I wondered if I should force-feed them fairy tales, threaten that if they did not listen to tales of winsome princesses and the intricate lacework of ancient legend they would be in sore need of magic the rest of their lives, but then I decided that there is magic in the foggy breath of trains and the machinations of numbers.

We went through a period where Malone, recently returned from Space Camp, wanted me to read him the list of astronauts who had flown missions. The list included all vital statistics — where they had been to college, how many missions they had flown, and their mission job descriptions. For me, it was excruciating, much like standing in line to fill out paperwork. For Malone, it was magical. All I had to do was mention an Apollo mission or the name of an astronaut he recognized, and he could see planets weaving their circle dances through space.

Recently, we have graduated to more interesting tales, and I delight in the voices the stories allow me—the ridiculously twisty addresses of Kipling ("Now, dearly beloved"), the whining self-absorption of Gub-Gub the pig, Gollum's sinister sneer.

I delight when I hear a soft, inadvertent chuckle from one of the boys. They are wrapped in storyland. They are listening.

It's not always easy. I am often tired at night, and I beg off more often than I would like to. Sometimes I don't beg off when I should.

I lay beside them the other night, too tired for the words on the page, my head ringing with an ear infection, trying to get Dr. Doolittle away from the clutches of the pirates and back home safely to England. As I read, my words trailed off into mumbles and sleep oozed from the corners of the room like ether. Finally I told them I couldn't read anymore because my ear hurt and I was tired.

"Why does your ear hurt, Mom?" Malone asked.

But by then the dreams had started in my head and I answered, "Capers and mushrooms."

They both digested that for a moment, then repeated. "Why does your ear hurt?"

"December 2nd," I answered.

Cameron woke me, falling out of the bed with laughter.

Malone simply shook his head.

"No, Mom," he said. "That's your birthday. You just lie there. I'll finish the chapter."

And he did. Sometimes, now, he reads to me, and Cameron lies with his face propped in his hands, listening without a hitch, all of us entranced with the Elephant's Child or the Pushme-pullyou.

But mostly we are entranced with one another.

I know somewhere inside that, although I have a love affair with words, it is not the words that count. The stories are wonderful, and the words are important. Read to your children, they say, and we scour the book shops and libraries for our favorite tales. We want to enrich our children's minds, stoke their imaginations, paint them bright pictures. We want, for them, the best.

But as I feel the growing bodies crowding what once seemed a spacious bed, the bodies still young enough to lean against me and curl around the stories, I realize that what we are doing is building more than their minds. Words and stories aside, it is the moment, the quiet in which the words flow, the reading light insulated by the dark room, the family tangled in a well-worn tale.

We are building their hearts.

Charlie

Charlie and I decided we'd call this story "Rumor Control."
Sometimes, when you feel like Wimberley's getting too big
for its cowboy boots, and you wonder what happened to the
sleepy little village you thought you'd moved to, do yourself a
favor: start a rumor. Make it a harmless one, so no one gets hurt.
Or go one step further and tell an interesting truth.

Your rumor will spread with the speed of a wildcat attack,
and the mildest kernel of truth will spring glowing up at you
out of the night with the crazed eyes of a wild animal.

Then you can breathe a sigh of relief and settle back into the
comfort of your small town, because nowhere but in a small
town does a rumor gain momentum with such imagination and
speed.

So let's set the rumor straight.

Charlie Davis, sculptor, carousel maker, storyteller, is heal-
ing nicely from his wounds. He'll even lift his shirt and show
you the three faint red scratches from the angry paw of a young
mountain lioness. They dug in deep enough to scare him and
shred the shirt his wife liked so much, but they did no real
harm.

And for those of you who might have heard otherwise,
Charlie did not visit the emergency room for mountain lion
wounds that fateful night, nor did he spend time in intensive
care.

And he knows you love him. The phone rang off the wall the following day. It seems everyone in town was worried about Charlie and called to see how he was doing, what kind of shape he was in.

Let's face it—there's something a little romantic about getting mauled by a mountain lion. It doesn't happen often, for one thing, and, for another, it has that primal quality of man pitted against nature. Though I'm not sure Charlie sees it that way.

Now, Charlie is no stranger to mountain lions. He's been around them all his life. Born in Henly, he was raised on the Fair Oaks Ranch near Boerne, where his father worked. Mountain lions weren't necessarily plentiful, he says, but they were there, and the ranchers didn't like them.

Mountain lions, Charlie explains, don't normally attack cattle or horses. They prefer venison, but, if old, wounded, or sick, they will treat themselves to an easier target and feast on livestock. Ranchers could care less about the nobility or majesty of the savage beast and shoot them whenever they have the chance.

He's heard them scream, he says, a bone-chilling experience that engraves itself in memory. A mountain lion screams to warn predators of its presence, and it sounds like a child being murdered, he says.

On a lighter note, mountain lions communicate with their cubs through whistlelike sounds, and when they're content, like any cat, they purr. The difference, says Charlie, is that they purr very loudly.

A little later in life, Charlie became acquainted with Shasta, the aging, cranky mascot at the University of Houston. Shasta, says Charlie, was bored. She didn't have anything to do, she was getting on in years, and she was tired of being bored, so she got cranky. Mountain lions will do that, Charlie says.

To alleviate her boredom, Shasta chewed the wooden door frame off the room she was kept in, and no one had the guts to go in and fix the door. Except Charlie. Charlie was on the staff at U of H, though he has a hard time explaining what his title was. He helped art students with their sculpting efforts, showing them how to put into practice what they had spent hours theorizing about in the classroom. He designed and built stage sets for the theater department. He worked with the art gallery setting up exhibits and displays. And he helped out the engineering staff.

Basically, he says, he was a hands-on kind of guy in a world of theorists, which might be why he was asked to climb into the lion's den and fix the door frame.

It was no problem, says Charlie. He simply entered Shasta's domain and threw her tether ball at her nose until she got cranky at it instead of him and sank her teeth into it. He then dragged her by the rope attached to the tether ball into another room, shut the door, and fixed the door frame, only this time he put in a metal door frame so he wouldn't have to do it again.

Then he left the U of H to help build 747s and jet hydrofoils, but that's probably not why.

So, you see, Charlie is no stranger to mountain lions.

Still, his past experiences didn't prepare him for what happened the other night. Let me give you a little background.

Charlie lives off Ranch Road 12 on the way to the junction, near his business, Carousels, Etc. His house is down in a valley, surrounded by two and a half to three miles of rugged wilderness, perfect mountain lion country. "It's remote," says Charlie, "wild, part of the Devil's Backbone."

He had seen the lioness and two small cubs for the first time about six months ago near a spring along Pierce Creek. Intrigued and a little bit pleased to see them, Charlie decided to leave them alone. They were no threat to him, and he was kind of glad to see them in this part of the country. They had been hunted for so long by ranchers, and their territory had been encroached on by houses, and they had become scarce, almost a legend in these parts. It's always nice to see a legend make a comeback.

Charlie saw them a few times after that and counted them as part of the wild fauna on his back forty.

A couple of weeks ago, he says, his neighbor decided to do a little clearing and burned some brush down in one of the canyons. Charlie figures the lioness was curious and had moseyed down to take a look at the clearing about the same time the neighbor had come to make sure the fire was out.

Probably, she was scared by the men, he says, and took a shortcut through Charlie's property to get home.

It was about 8:30 at night when Streaker started barking. Streaker is Charlie's black-and-white border collie, who runs around down in the canyons without any clothes on, Charlie says, and who is a coward. That's okay. Charlie likes her that way.

Anyway, Streaker started barking, and when Charlie opened the door to see what she was barking at, she barged past him into the house.

"I probably should've taken heed of what she did, because she ran into the house as soon as I opened the door," says Charlie.

Now apparently, Streaker is also acquainted with mountain lions. A while back, says Charlie, she came home from her run in the bottoms with puncture wounds in her hip. Something with sharp teeth had tried to take a taste of Streaker, but no one knew what was on the other end of those teeth.

Judging from the speed and determination of Streaker's entry into the house, Charlie has a better idea now.

So Charlie went out to investigate, carrying with him his little .22 pistol. He always carries that with him when he checks on his dog barking, he says. He's a long way from anything, and it's primitive out there.

The Johnson grass around Charlie's house is tall, maybe two or three feet, and dry from the freezes and the drought. Charlie crunched his way through it until, about fifty feet from his house, he saw the lioness's eyes flare out of the dark, and she was only six feet away.

It all happened pretty quick after that.

She was surprised and scared, Charlie says. He was, too.

"I was between her and the way out, and she looked at me and tried to make a hasty exit, but it was around or through me. She took a swipe at me in passing. It's amazing how fast you can suck in your gut."

Now, Charlie's gut is not formidable, but in the haste and fear of the moment, he didn't get it all the way sucked in, and she made contact.

As Charlie realized what was happening, as the cat launched herself into the air, as he stepped backward and sucked in his gut, he also fired at her five or six times with his .22 and didn't hit a thing.

We need to clear something up here. Charlie is not a lion hunter. He carves merry-go-round animals for children and whimsical adults. The animal heads that hang on his walls are fantasies carved of wood—dragon heads and unicorns. And it's a good thing. He's not a very good shot.

"She was just trying to get out of the way, and I just happened to be in the way," says Charlie. "But needless to say, I was a little bit excited."

Looking back at it, Charlie wishes he had it on video. He wishes someone had caught them both in midair as he fired five or six shots into the ground. They were both moving targets, but she had the better aim.

"It's funny now," he says, "but it wasn't funny then."

"Was she pretty?" I ask.

"I have no idea," says Charlie. All he remembers is her eyes flaring out of the night, a swath of tan fur coming at him, and her hindquarters as she cleared him. She wasn't very big, he says in retrospect, maybe fifty pounds and not much bigger than Streaker, who had wisely stayed in the house.

"And then," says Charlie, "I bravely ran away."

Actually, he says, he went back into the house to refuel, but, worried that he might have hit her and concerned about tracking a wounded mountain lion in the dark, he decided to call the game warden instead and look for her in the morning.

Morning came early, and with it came every kind of law-enforcement representative Charlie could think of. That was an experience, he says, to wake up to a bevy of officers on his doorstep.

But they soon thinned out to a deputy and a game warden and a guy named Tim Ajax, who works with Wildlife Rescue out of Comfort and has a tranquilizer gun. The idea, says Charlie, was to determine if she'd been wounded, and, if she had, to move her and her cubs to a mountain lion resort where they could be fed and rehabilitated.

But they found no blood. All they found were fresh tracks in the canyon dirt, evidence that she had probably moved her cubs deeper into the wild, distancing them from the menace she had encountered.

"Apparently," says Charlie, "I didn't hit a thing."

And Charlie's glad of that now. He doesn't mind sharing his acreage with a mountain lion family if they'll keep their distance, somewhere remote like Big Bend, Charlie says.

"I just don't like encountering them face to face in the wild," he explains.

But all in all, the scrape has given folks something a little different to talk about, and the rumor mill was harmless this time. Charlie probably can't remember the last time people were so eager to get a look at his stomach. It's a pretty good story.

Charlie sums it up well:

"She was scared, and I was scared, and we both got away."

There you have it.

# Garden

I'd been driving by the plant stand for days, for weeks, turning my head away from the bright tumble of flowers overflowing the pots; the tender shoots of chives and their pale, purple blossoms; the promise of pesto in the broad-leafed basil; the shy tomatoes, shouldering their way out of their small pots as if they did not have in them the cascading scarlet fruits of summer.

But finally, I couldn't stand it. I stopped the other morning and brought home some color. Not much, just enough to fill in the gaps in my terra cotta pots, just enough to placate myself with a small, feisty herb garden outside my kitchen door and a few flowers to remind myself of the earth.

I couldn't help it. With my windows open to the springtime, I could smell the wild onion and the honeysuckle. Sweetheart roses were peeking in my skylights. The mustang grape had climbed the cypress tree nearest my deck and was flirting its heady leaves and tendrils all over the morning air.

I used to have a garden in a former life, a big plot of land that was probably bigger than it needed to be, but, because I had it, I was greedy with the space.

It started with my love of tomatoes, my passionate involvement with summer's most dramatic fruit. While the first plants may seem small, innocuous, at best, they give way by June to performance art. They all but sing as they climb the silly confines of their cages and overflow the tops.

I have seen them overthrow the cages and crawl along the ground, like a child who refuses to be contained in a crib and ends up in the neighbor's yard while his mother is napping. They have minds of their own and sing arias while they spout out fruit, from the great pendulous ovals of plum tomatoes, to the globes and balloons and bursting red balls of celebrities and big boys.

They masquerade as grapes in clusters of sweet 100s, sweet 1,000s, red and gold confetti, summer's finest candy.

Like heartless sweethearts, they spark the passion of arguments: Who can grow the biggest and the sweetest? Which kind is the best? Is the old better than the new? Is mine better than yours? We come to verbal fisticuffs and love them all the more, our careless tomatoes, our summer fruit.

And when we harvest, we create bowls of color too lovely to eat sometimes, layering the blood red with fresh mozzarella and basil's greenest leaves. We blend together gazpachos, reaching through the cucumber vines for those slim, long companions, unsheathing the pungence of the garlic that marches in determined rows past the onions and the bright green purses of bell peppers.

Oh, I could sing the whole length of that garden, the love of tomatoes that trailed into sunflowers and Jerusalem artichokes and sweeping plots of black-eyed peas, the climbing curtains of perfumed sweetpeas infused with the sunrise, the feathers of the asparagus fronds.

I loved the way the zucchini metamorphosed from fingerling squash into baseball bats overnight like some alien growth in the garden. I loved how the zinnias came so willingly and gave and gave of their hot brilliance until the frost pulled its screen across the season.

I grew French haricots verts and Japanese eggplant, soybeans and purple beans, scotch bonnets and poblanos, crysanthemums and dahlias and crepe paper poppies. My babies chewed on tender okra as I carried their early, squirming weight in a backpack while I roto-tilled.

I loved to roto-till. Mechanically challenged by almost everything that sports a moving part, I could make the roto-tiller work and loved to see the weedy earth turn under on itself until I was closing in on solid black.

I hoed up rows for exotic potatoes and tried my hand at the wrought-iron fortitude of the artichoke plant. I softened the edges of the fence line in antique roses and populated one whole section of the garden in oregano and lemon balm. When I planted pincushion flowers one year, they came back unbidden, like lavender clouds.

It always threatened to overtake me, that garden. It was too big and too lavish, and while I worked on it with friends, it was always one leap ahead of our efforts. We only kept pace with it because we had faith, because we believed so fervently in its glory.

Even at its weediest, it produced and produced until we could hardly give away its bounty. And I couldn't stay away from generosity. At home, I loaded garbage cans with compost to give back some of what I had taken, my children's first lessons in recycling and the exchange of gifts.

I don't think I had a particularly green thumb, just a love of that green life, that undying holiday of color and taste.

Oh, it had its trying moments. One year, we tried to grow corn, and a late spring storm blew all the soldiers over at once. We covered more tomato plants than I care to count in cans and plastic and blankets and anything that would warm them against the uninvited freezes. A friend commented that if King Feed would begin selling tomato starts in January, they could make a killing.

We left the gate open and found deer bedded down in the black-eyed peas. We cried over a garden withered beyond hope when the well ran dry. We fought Johnson grass and nettle and puff adders and nests of newborn rabbits in the asparagus.

No matter the trial or triumph, I believe what that garden grew in me was a closeness to the earth. I felt the seasons move in my blood as they were turning in the wind. I felt the restless song of springtime and the close, packed earth of winter. I knew when the world was shifting its seasons. I was outdoors. I was a part of them.

And then life changed, as it will—unbidden and racing headlong into other venues. And that was not so bad, because changes can be as absorbing as the dreams they interrupt. But the garden fell by the wayside. I had no time for the continual weeds and watering. I had no time to watch the wet soil break open to the bent necks of slender seedlings. I had no time.

Then, the earth seemed far away. The seasons spun their cycles outside closed windows. Everything that grew in the open air seemed distant and muffled. When you have no time, the triumphs of the natural world seem as one-dimensional as postcards with no inscription on the back. Impersonal and mass-marketed. The world becomes homogenized when you move through it too quickly, and while the pictures change outside the windows, the internal temperature remains the same.

I have stopped by other people's gardens and admired. I have collected bags of compost leavings and given them to friends with gardens. I have bought flowers in the store and set them on my table. It's just not the same. I have missed the seasons filtering through my fingers. I have missed the rocks, the raw sunshine, the soft morning sun.

So last week, I bought some garden gloves and stuck them in a drawer. When I drove by the flower stand, I stopped and bought a flat of loopy purple cosmos and the tiny suns of wild zinnias. I bought a tall blue mealy sage plant and a whirling cherry splurge of dianthus.

When I finish this musing, I will pull on my new garden gloves and tuck the flowers between the herbs in my terra cotta plants, alongside the rosemary and the sage that weathered our mild winter last year.

Pots are a poor substitute for the movement of the earth, but the plants have it all figured out. They still quilt their colors through the season and relinquish to the frost. Though their yards may be small, they are rooted deeply in the soil.

In one of the pots, two tomato plants have dug in. I don't know what they are. A friend gave them to me because she had too many. I know their location is foolish. If they thrive, they will overcome the pots, tyrannize my gentle garden, rain tomatoes over all.

So maybe I will transport them into the real ground a little later. I still love tomatoes. I still believe in the seasons passing beneath my hands.

I have my eye on a small plot of dirt. Right now it is populated in fire ants and ambitious bamboo sprouts, but my tomatoes need space. And if I have tomatoes, I need cucumbers to keep them company in the gazpacho. I need basil, and what is a garden without zinnias? I need ... I need to feel the seasons shifting in my blood.

We must never lose the passion.

༄Back to School༄

It's happened again. I woke them up this morning, my boys, shook them from the cool, dark reaches of dreams and whispered into their sleepy ears, "Get up, guys! It's time for school. The first day of school. Remember?"

When I entered their room, the alarm was already beeping with all the effectiveness of a foghorn in a shipless sea. It had been beeping for at least fifteen minutes, and it took a lot of arm shaking, cajoling, and threatening on my part to effect the slow opening of an eye from at least one of the professional sleepers in the top bunk.

They've got this sleeping thing down, my boys, down to a fine art. They've been practicing all summer, developing a unique tandem style of approaching the night.

First, they would fight it, ignore it as if time and the lessening of daylight were a construct developed and implemented by parents. Regularly at about 3 P.M., one of them would ask me, What are we doing today? An hour or two later, Cameron, the seven-year-old, would ask me if he could have a friend over to play. When I tried to explain that the daylight was waning, and most of the day was gone, what we were doing for the day was mostly done, and it was a little late to invite a friend over, they would both stare at me in incomprehension.

We ate dinner late in the summer in an effort to escape the stultifying heat, so about 5 P.M., Cameron would usually ask

104

what we were having for lunch. When I reminded him that he had already eaten lunch, he would say he thought that was breakfast. Reminding him that he had risen from sleep only in time to eat a midday meal just served to confuse the issue.

When dinner finally arrived, in whatever form it took, they usually weren't hungry, the starvation cramps that had plagued them earlier now mere memories.

And if hunger was not an issue, neither was sleep. They were not of the school where nighttime betokened rest or sleep. With no schedules to tangle with the freedom of their lives, they saw no need to apply the rules of sunrise and sunset. If I refused to comply with the potential offered by electric lights past the random hour of 11 P.M. or even midnight—well, they could see just fine in the dark. And anyone knows that the lack of light inspires conversation.

Many a summer night, I walked past their room late to hear the muffled voices of young boys, earnest and soft, punctuated in their low music by howls of laughter.

"Go to sleep!" I would bark, and they would fall into an immediate and suspect silence. If I waited long enough in the dark hallway, I would hear the voices start again and continue until they began to lift the edges of sleep, like something small and soft slipping beneath the satin binding of a blanket.

Sometimes, I wished I could have heard their meanderings. What kind of secrets do a seven- and ten-year-old pass between them? What information is shared and embellished and stored in their opening minds?

And at night, after a day of jousting and sparring, of arguing, pinching, and poking, they would climb into the same bunk, these two rivals. They would put the day aside so that at night, they might feel the comfort of a brother in the dark. If a friend spent the night, the muffled talks stretched well past any sensible hour, and even I could not outlast them in the hallway.

So of course they slept late. And I let them, for isn't that why God invented summer in the first place? Isn't summer the loosening of the rules? Isn't summer the wide-flung luxury of boredom and indolence? Isn't summer all about sleeping in—at least when you're young?

In the mornings, they slept with a kind of heady determination. I loved to watch them. They looked as if they had dug in deep beneath the dark turf of sleep. They worked at it. It was a concentration of dreams, a tour de force of blankness. These boys were professional sleepers, and when they woke, they were tired from the effort.

So waking them this Thursday for that first day of school was not easy. I had to mention words like *shower* and *breakfast* and *backpack* and *late.* These are not summer words, and with the heat still pressing at the windows and threatening the day, it seemed strange to bring them out, like stout woolens from a foreign season, and try them on for size.

But the alarm clock beeped, and they stirred and moaned and raised their fair heads from their pillows and burrowed back in. I reminded them that they would see friends, they would wear new clothes, they would have fun, and they dug themselves back out and inched their way toward the shower. Half an hour later, I found them huddled under towels, crouched on the floor like conspirators.

"What are you doing?" I asked. "You're going to be late for school!"

They pondered the meaning of those words as if trying to recall the lyrics to a distant song and moved slowly toward the pile of new clothes. Malone, the ten-year-old, had carefully selected his outfit for the first day of school. A fifth-grader, he is mastering a growing awareness of the rest of the world. I see it in his stance—hands on his slim hips, head held high, a kind of adolescent indifference draped cautiously over his natural curiosity. Colors match better when he pulls them from the drawer, and both socks are the same length on his brown legs.

Cameron probably would have been content to go to school in nothing but his new tennis shoes. Clothes are a dispensable commodity to him, and the shoes only mattered because they were new. They won't be next week, and, chances are good they'll be lost.

And then we gathered school supplies. We had bought them earlier in the week, roaming the aisles of Wal-Mart along with all the other lost souls in the world of plethora. Too many choices. Too many different colored binders, erasers, school supply boxes, notebooks.

All the way to the store they had listened to Billy Idol, a loud, throat-tearing musician of whom both boys are enamored. I had listened to them listening to Billy Idol, marveling at the way Cameron could replicate the hiss and click and thump of the percussion instruments with faultless timing as I tried to ignore the raucousness of the music.

When we found the school supply section at Wal-Mart, Malone made a beeline for the binders and returned with a black, zippered binder clutched to his chest and his eyes wide with pleading.

"Please, Mom," he begged. "This is the perfect binder. It's so cool. Could we please get this binder."

After the Billy Idol session, I was almost afraid to look. What kind of binder would a Billy Idol fan choose?

He held it out to show me Garfield the cat clawing his way out of the fabric cover.

"It's Garfield, Mom. He's so cool. I just love him. Don't you?"

"Yes, my love," I said. "He is *so* cool."

I wanted to cry. I looked at the handsome blond boy in front of me and saw him straddling two sides of the fence, as yet unaware of the fence. Life is full of fences that have to be climbed, of incongruities and mismatched perceptions, of Billy Idol and Garfield.

I bought him the Garfield binder gladly, more than willing to sustain the innocence that inspired his love of the temperamental cat. On the way home, we discussed the nature of cats and forgot all about Billy Idol.

So with Garfield packed inside Malone's backpack and new shoes lightening Cameron's step, we broke the easy heat of summer with routine. It's not unwelcome. A steady diet of dessert becomes cloying after a while, and structure is what creates the beauty of freedom.

Malone walked onto the Bowen Middle School campus with his head held high, his hair combed just so in front and rumpled in the back. He forgot his locker combination, and I had to retrieve it from the car. He held my hand until we had his classroom in our sights. Then he casually, but deliberately, dropped it.

Cameron sprinted from the car to the sidewalk, almost forgetting his school supplies in his eagerness. He threw himself into

Principal Tucker Blythe's arms and danced toward the second-grade hall at Scudder Elementary. I followed and tried to swallow the growing lump in my throat.

The boys are gone, and the house is quiet. I no longer have to think about what we are doing today or who can come over and play. The door to the outside remains shut most of the day, and the milk stays in the refrigerator.

It's afternoon, and the quiet is becoming louder. It's ten minutes 'til school lets out, and I can't wait.

 Flood

I woke a week ago Thursday to the sounds of rain. Nothing new. It had been raining since Easter. You know Texas weather—83 degrees and cloudless skies one day with heartfelt promises of an early summer. The next day, when we go out to check on the progress of the Easter Bunny, 60 degrees, misting, and a springtime assurance of rain and rampant greenery.

It was so damp on Easter, the egg dye was coming off on our hands as we tried to eat our way through all the hard-boiled eggs we could stomach, as the kids stomped through the weed-high grass beneath the cascading wisteria, complaining they were cold, and someone had more eggs than someone else, and that person was getting more help from the neighbors, who *somehow* knew where all the eggs were hidden.

It was so damp, we might have called it rain if we weren't trying to pretend that it really wasn't going to rain on Easter because we were attending an al fresco Easter dinner that was too big to be moved inside, and maybe if we didn't call it by its name, it wouldn't behave like the rain it was fixing to become.

We did eat outside, weathered the dampness, and commented, to the person, how, after last year's parchment paper skies and arid lawns, after the early heat and the late heat, and the reticent springs and the receding river, we weren't going to complain about a little dampness.

Which was a good decision, as the rain continued through

the week as if it had always been there, as if it were just as familiar with these Texas skies, this rough terrain, as it had ever been. As if, just a few nights earlier, these skies hadn't been so clear and so cloudless you could see the comet splashed across the night like a spray of glitter on a black velvet painting.

No, last week was all gray and rainy, green and rainy, gray and green and wet. The dampness was solid, never let up, but the rain was light and timid. None of the driving force that floods things. No fury or threat or raging storm.

It was frustrating, in a way. The earth was muddy and entered the house unbidden on the bottoms of shoes and the feet of dogs. The wood in the woodpile grew ripples of brilliant fungus and refused the flame when prodded with a match. The ground grew soggier underfoot, but, thirsty as it could be, continued to drink the light rain as if it could not get enough, a thirst starved by years of drought and too many straws in the glass.

Then, Thursday night, the damp turned to rain in earnest, and I lay in bed and thought, *This is the rain that floods things.* And then I prayed, *Let this be the rain that floods things.*

It drummed through the night at the doors and the windows. It knocked the petals from my sweetheart roses and laid the tall grasses low with the weight of its presence. It unfurled the green from the tight-fisted cypress along the creek and puddled down the road in murky pools.

First thing, I checked in early light for flooding, stood at the bedroom window and watched the creek, which was up, but not overly up, which headed downstream with a contained enthusiasm. I grabbed a cup of coffee and headed across the road to see if the river had sprung itself from its banks, but it mulled and roiled softly, a milk-chocolate brown slipping through the safety of its channel.

When I came back from taking the children to school, the rain had let up, a dream of drumming from the night before, and the river had begun to grow. Thirsty or sated, the earth can only drink so much. The Blanco was leaving its banks. I strolled with my dog, who has not dried out in weeks, to see what I thought would be the drama of the creek merging with the river, but the waters were so backed up and muddy, we could not distinguish one from the other, and the flat white rocks where we lay last summer watching the water waste away were gone, not even shadows under the rising river.

By the time we retraced our steps to the house, a small crowd had gathered on the river bluff to watch the growing flood. We stood in the damp smell of cedar and mud and watched chairs float by, lumber, inner tubes, a large inflated plastic hand, trees, fence posts, and whatever else had been caught unprepared for the flood.

My dog sat beside me, his head turning to follow each large object as it floated by. Dedicated to year-round swimming, he looked confused. His swimming hole had changed complexion, changed beyond recognition. He wasn't going to chance it, but if the waters didn't drop, it looked to be a long, hot summer.

I live on the peninsula where the river and creek merge their waters, surrounded almost by a constant flow, and the energy of the flood filled that Friday like a tangible presence, a taste in the air, a pulsing forward of more than the water, a gateway to spring.

We have needed this flood. Our waters have followed the rule too well, stayed within the confines of their curves too long. Rules must be tested on occasion, reconsidered, reconstructed, or they grow stale. The long green moss accumulates on the bottom of the river, and silt collects in more than just the hollows. The river begs for cleaning. The river cries for flood.

And so the rains were more than welcome. I've seen bigger floods, more devastation, a current that wouldn't die down for weeks, but few floods that were more welcome. The river settled back into its banks after its spree, and all day and all night it sang its deep brown song. It flowed through more rain, through high winds and lightning, and still it covered rocks we had come to accept as riverbank.

The next day, the light broke a blue sky, as blue as any spring sky might dream of becoming in the deadest of winter dreams. It was a fairy-tale day, all panpipes and birdsong and lute strings in the moving air. We walked along the riverbank through grasses and wildflowers bent by the waters and rising back toward the sun. We strolled through slender onions, their pearls unearthed, fragrant and shining in the sunlight.

Where the creek joined the river, the light fell through leaves like liquid, and the creek's clear water tumbled and frothed toward that brown journey below. The river was baritone and bass, serious as a bulldozer. The creek was soprano, dressed in a tutu, a giddy and frivolous harmony.

Oh, it was spring last weekend, all weekend long. It was so soft and sweet, it was shiny. After days of rain and gray, of drizzle and mud, it was more than we thought we could ask for.

The children abandoned the television and the beeping of electronic games to gather armfuls of spring onions. They waded in the creek and crawled beneath the waterfall on the dam. They picked me wildflowers and rode their bicycles through the mud puddles on the street, spattering brown stains up the backs of their shirts. They couldn't get enough of the sunlight. Neither could I.

And now it's gone. Again. I know I can't complain. I remember last summer. I remember the thirst. And I know these dark skies breed a bluer blue, a deeper green. I know they forestall the heat. I know they are the gray velvet curtains of spring.

Cultural Diversity

A speech given at Wimberley High School,
Cultural Diversity Day, Cinco de Mayo 1996

Because I have written a book on the history of Wimberley, and history drags culture along behind it like a little red wagon, I have been asked to speak on cultural diversity in Wimberley. We become who we are by living, and our lives create the history we leave behind. They also create the patterns on which our children build their lives, and that is our culture.

The first definition of *culture* in the dictionary is the appreciation and understanding of literature, arts, and music. The second is the customs and civilization of a particular people or group. While the second definition might seem to better apply to what we're talking about today, I think we would be missing something important to skim too quickly over the first.

To me, the key words in the first definition are *appreciation and understanding*. What follows those words are *literature, arts, and music*. Those are the spirit and soul of a culture. The arts are where we express ourselves, where our desires and fulfillments and frustrations climb out of their cages and paint canvases and walls, fill rooms with songs and the swirling spirals of dance, press language into the acrobatics of poetry and the fascination of folk- and fairy tales.

Art breaks down barriers. While we may not understand the language of another culture, we hear in their music something that talks to us, even though that music is nothing like the music we hear when we turn the knob to the local radio station. Maybe you like to listen to George Strait, Pearl Jam, Boyz to Men, or the Eagles. Maybe you've never heard the kind of music Correo Aereo plays. But my guess is that if you open your mind and your heart just wide enough to let a little of that unfamiliar music in, you'll hear something that part of you responds to. You'll hear, appreciate, and perhaps start on the path of understanding another culture.

Music is not all. Sometimes it's artwork that makes you turn back and take a second look, that speaks to you in a language that has more to do with similarity than diversity. Or maybe it's the differences that catch your eye. Maybe you fall in love with the broad, bright colors of the Mexican muralists or the earth-toned geometry of African design.

Differences can close doors if you are frightened by those differences. Listen to that African drumbeat. If you feel that the different rhythm in the music threatens your own musical style, you can turn the knob on the radio, and you may never see the jungles of the world.

Or you can turn up the volume and listen carefully. You might get a few ideas that you incorporate into your own style, ideas that stretch your way of thinking, that feed you with the foods of diversity.

And what a restaurant. Pizza and stromboli, salsa and mole, sushi and sashimi, Peking duck and hot and sour soup, Irish soda bread, Boston baked beans, Navajo fry bread, crawfish pie and filé gumbo, fried chicken and cream gravy. The menu is incredible, the choices endless. Explore the menu of cultural diversity, but watch out. You may find yourself putting jalapeños on your next hamburger or soy sauce in your fajita marinade.

We are a mix of cultures, whether we want to admit it or not. People like to say—some with pride, some with embarrassment— that Wimberley ranks low on the chart of cultural diversity.

I hesitate to call myself a historian, since dates and details of

chronology often leave my head as soon as I have committed them to paper. But I do retain the big picture. Looking back across the years I wrote about, I can see the speck of dust that caught the tumbleweed that rolled into town yesterday as a Mack truck hauling lumber materials for the umpteenth spec home going up in Woodcreek tomorrow.

There is an element of truth in saying we lack cultural diversity. We do not claim a wide range of ethnic variation in this small town. Minorities, unlike in many small towns in Texas or big cities anywhere, are truly in the minority here. Not to say they aren't here. We have a representation of every race here, I imagine, but we don't wage the big battles of fear and oppression that bloody so many areas.

Why that is, I'm not sure. Wimberley, like anywhere else, has its prejudices and always has. If you are part of an ethnic minority, you may feel some of that. You may also feel the acceptance that comes from the close ties of a small community that accepts and loves its own.

No, the differences we have in this town tend more toward differences in lifestyle and beliefs, and those have been here since Wimberley first started to grow.

Some say Wimberley is a spiritual place, a place that welcomes a holiness that has many names and labels. Indians recognized it and set up camp under the green sway of cypress and tumbling waters. They left enough evidence behind— arrowheads, spear points, burned rocks—that we can imagine their dreams, their love of this land.

White settlers moved here in the early 1800s and anchored their dreams to the thin soil with houses and mills and family names, some of which are still around. They persisted through droughts and floods and the invasion of an aerial army of grasshoppers that ate everything they tried to grow. They loved this land enough to stay.

They grew cotton and corn, cattle and angora goats. They raised educators and hermits, spinsters and mothers of dynasties, drunkards and preachers, artists and electricians, and cedar choppers and musicians. They loved and they hated, worked themselves to the bone and danced 'til the sun came up in the morning. They prayed under grape arbors and hunted 'coons under the full moon.

If there was a sameness to them, it was in their persistence and their dedication to the land we live on now. Some of those old families are still here. But most of us are newcomers. We are here because we choose to be.

We come from all over, and we bring with us our own histories, our own way of doing things. We bring with us our culture. The differences might not be as glaring as skin color or language, but they are here.

Since people moved into this valley, they have brought with them the richness of diversity, the beauty of a crazy quilt, like a map sewn with satins and calicos, corduroys and cottons, burlap and silk. A crazy quilt hinges on scraps of memories and, to me, is the most beautiful of all quilts because it doesn't work off a pattern, but takes its wholeness from the flexibility of the different pieces of fabric.

When tourists found Wimberley, think of the diversity they brought in—a more moneyed way of life, the experience of travel, the freedom of mobility. They introduced artists to the area, and the artists walked into that spirit we call Wimberley and painted it and sang to it and lived in the midst of it and loved it.

Sixty years ago, during the Great Depression, this town bred the spirit of Kim Tinney, who lived in a hole in the ground and hauled rattlesnakes to town in a burlap bag. Some people called him Wimberley's first hippie. In the summer, he slept in the river and covered himself with a buffalo hide to keep the minnows away. He hitched rides into town and announced himself by jumping off the tailgate of the truck and bellowing his arrival. By many accounts, he was the first person in Wimberley to wear shorts, and he did that without the benefit of a dress code. He was a character. He was unique. And he was accepted. Self-respecting families fed him dinners and listened to his stories when he felt like telling them.

Wimberley nurtured the spirit of Buck Winn, international muralist, painter, architect, and sculptor, who moved here from the big city of Dallas and created monumental sculptures in the cedar brakes. He brought to these hills a different kind of culture—the furious drive and the playful whimsy of creativity. He was a character. He was unique. And he was accepted by a people who might have been more comfortable with Kim Tinney's eccentricities than those of the big city artist. Though Buck died more than a decade ago, his workshop still stands, and people can tour it to see the accomplishments and follies of a truly creative mind.

Wimberley weathered the freedoms of the '60s and the '70s, the whirlwind financial changes of the '80s, and it is feeling its way through the growth of the '90s. Artists flock here. Musicians sing between these hills. Belly dancers snake their way through our festivals and two-steppers sand the floors of the local dance floors with their boots, while the local cafe serves up Greek salads, vegetarian tacos, and thick, rare steaks.

We have a freedom here. We mix the very young and the very old. We mix our social climates. In many ways, we are very, very lucky. Go to a Wimberley function, and you will find the man with the big green lawn sharing a drink with the man who cuts it, both roaring over a joke and a plate of barbecue or pie.

This is a town that has, in so many ways, dropped its barriers. That is why we live here. It's not for the money we can make. It's for the lifestyle we can claim and the freedoms we can have.

That does not mean we become irresponsible and step on the rights of others. It means we appreciate and understand the differences. The potentials here are unlimited. We are a small enough town that each one of us can have a voice that can be heard. People know who we are. We care about each other.

What a gift we have been given. We are never too young or too old to enjoy it, to learn from it.

Close no doors. Listen to your neighbor's music. Try his cooking. Share your poetry and your artwork with him. Play with his children. You may find he has opened your mind, and you may find you have given him a gift he could find nowhere else.

Cinco do Mayo is a celebration of freedom. I say celebrate the differences in our culture, and, in them, find the similarities that bind us all to where we are and join our hands in friendship.

Scout Camp I

I am sitting in the early-morning light surrounded by piles of clothing, a footlocker, a duffel bag, a sleeping bag, stationery, cowboy boots, hiking boots, river shoes, a lariat, science fiction novels, and a small plastic tub of Jelly Bellys.

How did it come to this? Is this what it means to grow up — that you consent to your worst dreams in order to enrich the lives of your children? That you agree to pack them for camp?

My eleven-year-old is leaving me for a pretty good stint of time. He's flying the friendly skies north for the breathtaking coolness of the Tetons, where he will learn to throw the lariat and ride horses and fly-fish and mountain climb. He is taking long underwear and fleece jackets and wool socks and three blankets. His sleeping bag will keep him warm to 15 degrees.

I am sweating. The sun is barely up, and I am already sweating and crying small, private tears that I hope he will not see, because no one likes to see their mother cry.

I eye the duffel bag. It's big and black and waiting to be stuffed. I wonder, briefly, if I could fit inside.

I never liked packing for camp, and as I stuff the foam pad into the duffel, realizing that it leaves little space for anything else, I wonder if he will be able to repack what I have so neatly laid out for him when camp is over.

I never liked packing for camp, I remember, as I write his

name on the underwear that missed out on the first phase of labeling. I never liked that scary feeling that I had forgotten something crucial or that I would run out of clothes or they wouldn't be the right ones or I would be too hot (I never was worried about being too cold). I never liked packing for camp.

But here I am, awake before anyone else so I can pack my son for camp and cry privately before he wakes up.

It's a wonderful experience he's headed off to, my slender, blond, brown-eyed boy who dreams of being an astronaut and patiently explains the lives of appliances to me when I am about to buckle with the frustration of a technology-driven world.

It's a wonderful gift of the outdoors and the animals and a season of summer boys. I can see them in the cold water, soaring from rope swings, diving from cliffs. I can see them riding their horses through the tall grass and wildflowers of early summer, crouched around the gold of a campfire at night.

I impress on him the importance of eating, reminding this very cerebral child that food sustains the mind. Indeed, food sustains life. And I won't be there to impress that upon him at mealtime.

I ask him to write me letters that tell me how he feels, as well as what he's doing. I buy him the Ray Bradbury books I loved at his age in hopes that he might find the time to read them.

I sense only the great adventure ahead of him until the morning he leaves, and then the world crowds in. What if he doesn't like it up there? What if he doesn't get along with the other campers? What was I thinking to let him leave for so long at such a young age? Will he ever be old enough for me to let him go without crying?

It's every mother's fear, every parent's fear, I know.

He has been strolling through the house in his cowboy boots and hiking boots for days, trying them on with different pairs of jeans, tilting the new straw hat just so.

Our cowboy friend loaned him his lariat and even gave him lessons in the driveway. We averted a crisis when he discovered that throwing that rope wasn't as easy as it looked. Tears of frustration were creeping in when I explained to him that he was going to camp to learn. They didn't expect him to arrive a seasoned cowboy. He had to leave them some room to teach him something. I don't think he was convinced, but he coiled the rope up and put it in his footlocker for later.

He seems so confident, strolling off in his big boots to the other side of the country, but I remember how I felt as left the temperate zone of northern California for the banks of the Guadalupe River and Camp Arrowhead every summer. I approached it with a sense of exhilaration, laced with dread. The chemistry of camp is a little different every year, and one never knows the mix at the outset.

I can't tell him my fears, and he won't tell me his. Afraid I'll start crying, probably, but he confides in my sweetheart that he is scared, and he holds on to us a lot these past few days.

His younger brother rolls his eyes and says, "Oh, great! Mom's gonna start crying at the airport again." There is nothing quite like the disgust of an eight-year-old.

So I reorder what I can of his domestic universe. Scattered as my own life is, I feel the need to send him off with some semblance of order in his. I know it won't come back ordered, and I wonder if maybe I shouldn't send along an extra duffel bag so he can fit in the clothes that seem to grow toward the end of camp, that develop minds of their own and refuse to fit into the space in which they arrived.

But he will have to learn that, I guess, the same way he learns to throw a lariat.

He is awake now and hugging on the small black lab who will seem full-grown when he returns. He wants to take her with him. "No," I tell him. "They specifically said no dogs. No dogs and no moms."

So I will let him go with what grace I can muster. I will open my hands because I'm afraid of squeezing too hard. I know that he will dazzle them at camp. I know his horse will carry him well. I know he will be able to lasso any cedar stump he wants when he comes home. I know he will eat.

Everything barely fits into the footlocker and the duffel bags, but it fits.

My heart is expanding in my chest, and the tears are circling the campfire.

Go, my gift. Make it a summer you will always remember. Make the dreams inherent in those big boots and that coiled rope come true. Let the mountains pull you high. Let the waters cool you. Let the horses lope beneath your young body like the wind. Write me long letters and come home with stories. Sing and dream and laugh.

Teach me how to let you go.

༄࿇࿇ Scout Camp II ༄

I remember well the last-minute packing, the search for the missing soap dish and the batteries for the flashlight. I remember the musty canvas smell of the dull green army surplus duffel bag pulled from beneath the bed or from the recesses of the limitless attic.

I remember packing the stupid thing, my mother and I neatly folding my little-girl shirts, then wadding them into unrecognizable shapes and shoving them into the netherworld that was the far end of the duffel bag. I remember writing my name in indelible ink on everything.

The sleeping bag I took to camp had been my father's in a more military period of his life. It, too, was army green and heavy with goose down, a soft and solid protection against the night mists of the redwood forests of Pescadero, California, where Camp Skylark was summer home to hundreds of Girl Scouts.

I packed sweatshirts and hiking boots, stationery and insect repellent. I packed a tight fist of anticipation and a clinging hand that dreaded leaving the high ceilings and wide windows of my home on Pepper Lane.

But for several years I made that brief, odd journey where we left the safety of our parents for counselors, whom we called something other than their real names. I wandered through the fern forests and learned the fine art of lashing sticks together with rope. I sang many rounds with many other voices, learning words to songs I haven't heard since and still find myself humming in random moments. I learned how to use an outhouse in the pitch black of night and how to raise a flag in a meadow stunned with the dew and the early-morning light.

I don't have daughters. I have sons. So when they came of a certain age, I duly enrolled them in Cub Scouts, hoping to anchor a kind of American tradition to their growing bones. And I suppose I have.

Last week, my youngest, my seven-year-old wild man, helped me stuff a few items into a duffel bag, purchase flashlight batteries and insect repellent, and head off for Scout camp.

Only this isn't northern California, and as we drove toward the Dripping Springs Horse Center Scout Camp, through the heat-seared fields of the Hill Country, I decided we were a very long way from the mists of the redwood forests. There was no sweatshirt in the duffel bag, no down in the sleeping bag.

I had volunteered to spend the first night with the cubs from our troop, providing additional support for Scoutmaster Tom Bauman, a brave man if ever there was one, until relief support could show up the second day and I could return to the workaday world.

So I also had my own small duffel bag tucked into the back of the car and a well-worn green tent that had seen more than a few camping trips and held a kind of graceful sway in its stance, something along the lines of the Arabian Nights in miniature.

Cameron, my son, was so excited he was directionless. He had watched his older brother go to camp, but had been too young to stray from home before this summer. He had yearned for the independence of summer camp, and I worried that my presence might hold him back or fetter the freedom of his flight.

Needless concerns. I think he was glad to have me along, although when we set up our small tent, and he saw the big, airy tent that sheltered the other four boys, he elected to sleep with them.

"Is that okay, Mom?" he asked solicitously. "Will you be okay by yourself? Do you mind?"

I looked at our small, sway-backed tent and tried to envision two bodies packed closely, side by side, in the stifling heat. I remembered how he tossed and turned in the night and how the waffled foam we had brought to soften the heat-packed earth was only large enough for one and a half bodies, and I gave him my blessing.

I would be okay, I told him. I was not afraid to sleep by myself. And besides, I was only about fifteen feet from where he would be sleeping in case I got scared.

"Good," he said, "because me and the other guys are going to tell ghost stories."

"Great," I said.

We started off the camp with a swimming test—or tried to. We joined about fifty other Scouts and their parents in a line-standing exercise in the heat of the 5 P.M. sun. Cameron didn't mind so much, because he kept cool by racing in and out of the nearby showers, something he usually avoids at all costs. I had not dressed in my swimsuit, because I didn't plan to have my swim skills tested, so I felt awkward about running in and out of the showers with the Cub Scouts.

Instead, I stood in line, something I hate as much as Cameron hates to take a shower. In fact, I told myself, that's why I live in the country—so I don't have to stand in line.

After about half an hour, I had traveled two feet forward, and I—like the fathers around me—was hot. We weren't telling ghost stories, and while we were trying to be amiable, we were not amused. Mostly, we were just really, really hot.

So I broke line and headed up to the pool area to see what was going on. Fortunately, the pools were small, but only one child at a time could be tested because there was only one lifeguard. As I came upon the scene, a young blond boy had lowered himself into the water and was gamely making for the other side, which was about fifteen feet away.

"See?" he said. "I can swim just fi—."

I never caught the rest of what he was saying, because he said it underwater. When he resurfaced, he had swallowed part of the pool and was having trouble talking. But he was still headed for the far end of the pool in a fashion that bore a distant resemblance to swimming.

"We've been here for an hour," one mother behind me confided, "and we've only moved about four feet. If I were you, I'd come back tomorrow."

The lifeguard looked my way briefly and nodded—vigorously.

"Great idea," I said and hauled a protesting Cameron off toward the campground to suit up for the flag ceremony.

"But Mom," he hollered. "I want to swim!"

"Later," I said. "You can swim later. Right now, you have to get dressed up for a flag ceremony."

"What's that?" he asked.

My head spinning from the heat, all I could think of to say was, "You'll see."

Soon, Mr. Bauman and I had the Scouts outfitted in their blue and gold, and we were headed for the flagpole. What followed was so reminiscent of my Scouting days, I could have cried. The backdrop was different, all scrub cedar and dried grass, but the songs were just as silly, and the enthusiasm among the young counselors ran just as high.

I watched my small, wayward troop adjust itself to the idea of pomp and circumstance—their blue uniform shirts smartly buttoned to the neck, their gold Scout scarves unfurling from the Bobcat emblem. Beneath the shirts, they wore swimsuits and cutoffs and cowboy boots and tennis shoes without socks. It didn't matter. They were dressed to kill.

After all the introductions and pranks—the counselors racing forward to pull down the camp director's socks ("Why did they do that, Mom?")—they herded us toward the mess hall, which was right next to the horse arena.

Cameron and another friend struck out in front. Mr. Bauman's son held his father's hand and confided as how they were buddies. ("We've been buddies a long time," Mr. Bauman agreed.) And the blond twin brothers, whose names no one could get straight, drifted, as they did all weekend, like small leaves caught in a wind. Quiet and individual as a team, they slipped easily from sight, bent on their own thoughts and directives, so that always we were calling, "Alex! Ben! Stay put!"

After dinner, where we had the kind of discussions about manners I am beginning to think are germane to all seven-year-olds, we toured the camp, learning the rules of the BB range and the archery range, the landmarks of the BMX bike track, and the warnings about the horses.

As a child, I had always been in love with horses, and given a choice between a horse and a bike, I would have jumped on a horse any day, but I could see the boys' eyes light up when they saw the bike track. As they raced their way on foot around the berms built for jumping, I could see their inner visions, their ambition to go airborne on the seat of those small bikes.

The Cubs weren't the only ones. A father raised his hand and asked the instructor if the parents could ride too.

"You bet," she said. "If you want to."

Later in the evening, the staff composed campfire skits for us, with the light of the campfire coming from spotlights, the burn ban having quenched the embers of any real flames.

"Where is the fire?" Cameron kept asking, leaning his tired head against my shoulder. "I don't see any campfire."

But what I heard that night is what tradition is made of. Many of the campers were on their first camping expedition and didn't know what to expect. Others were veterans. But the parents knew the songs and the hand motions to the songs, and the words to Taps. And those parents, who had taken time off from work to accompany their children, were determined that some experiences be shared and continued. They were tying onto the anchor in the midst of a swirling stream, and they planned to leave their children with traditions to pass along to their children. In a flash card world, it is the thin threads of culture that gift us with any continuity, with any lifeline from which we feel safe to stray.

So as the evening deepened and the children yawned, I watched the parents—many in Scouting uniforms—marshal their small troops back to the tents, and as Mr. Bauman and I stood outside the Porta-Potties trying to keep up with five small and wandering spirits, I wondered how many ghost stories were unraveling in the tents beneath the shadowy glow of flashlights that night.

We dispensed toothpaste and admonished the boys about noise and the value of sleep, and I crawled into my billowy shelter and listened to the night.

It was a long one. A fine, strong wind sailed through at one point and threatened to lift me from the ground, tent and all, and occasional prickly rain slanted through the tent opening. But I think I slept, and the boys thought they did, too.

I left the next morning after a flag ceremony and a sturdy breakfast. I stayed long enough to see them through arts and crafts, where they learned the fine art of sharing tools. When I climbed in the car, they were gathered around the flagpole, learning how to conduct a flag ceremony.

Cameron had held tight to my arm, and I could see his career in independence taking a dubious turn, but he weathered it.

When I left, the boys looked small, grouped around Mr. Bauman, their heads tilted back to watch the flag. Idyllic as that scene might sound, I knew better. I knew Cameron was saying, "Why are we doing this?" Aaron was probably poking Ben, who was dreaming of drifting down the field to play with some rocks he'd seen on his way over to the flag, and Alex would be drifting right behind him. Erik would be standing by his father and talking a blue streak. And all of them couldn't wait to get to the BMX bicycles and the BB range.

I loved it. I wish I could've stayed.

Cold

Well, we made it through the cold and have emerged on the other side as survivors of an ordeal.

Think about it. For days, the one topic of conversation you could count on was the weather—how cold it was, and how cold it was going to get. Lesser conversations, like side dishes to the main course, focused on breaking pipes, projected electric bills, and cabin fever.

It came as a surprise. The Farmer's Almanac projected balmy days and clear skies for the beginning of February. The big-town newspaper forecast a cooling trend toward the end of the week, but by midafternoon Tuesday, a friend called to tell me it was getting cold and was supposed to get colder. In fact, she said, we were in the direct path of an arctic front that was blowing Eskimos in front of it, snowdrifts that would bury a tall man, icy silver winds that carried winter in their breath.

I have to admit I got a little bit excited. Winter had been a stranger this year—elusive, shy, unwilling to commit. The grasses are as gold from lack of rain as they are from the occasional midnight romp into the upper 20s. I still had coats and sweaters encased in last year's plastic cleaning bags. No need to take them out. On my birthday in early December, the high peaked somewhere in the 80s. Children waded in the river, and we moved into the night in short-sleeved shirts.

So when winter finally promised an appointment, I had an

open slot. I was ready for a change, knowing it would be brief and I would be ready for it to be over by the time it left.

I think everyone was ready for a change. What we were not ready for was the chaos that ensued.

We all have dreams of winter. The good dreams are warmed by fireplaces with oak flames, fed by steaming bowls of spicy chili. In those dreams, we gather our families and friends together to watch movies at home. We wrap ourselves in blankets, snuggle into the soft warmth of down comforters, and sleep the long white sleep of winter, dreamless inside the dream. We wake late and watch the gray light at the windows slide along the icy crystal coating on the trees. We watch the water breathe its lingering breath, and we snuggle in deeper, insular in our warmth, protected.

Those are the dreams we share.

And then there are the bad dreams. Bad dreams live in frozen pipes and slide like nightmares on the dark glass of icy streets, past the stalled, broken cars. They chill beneath the bone, a cold that no oak flames can warm.

Bad dreams dance to the acid rock of screeching cars, metal against metal, tires locked on ice. They breathe a labored breath, a congestion of sharp, hard-edged air that forces through sneezes and reddened, stopped-up noses.

Bad dreams chap the hands and whistle through the cracks in walls, climbing out through the last of the firewood, the shadows of everything we meant to do and didn't get around to.

Those are the dreams we'd like to forget.

A combination of those dreams fed the chaos. It started Thursday morning with the call from the schools. Having just forfeited one of their bad-weather days to good weather the week before, the schools were closing shop, sending the kids home early, afraid that dire forecasts would prove true and school buses would lock up on frozen roads in the afternoon or early mornings.

At Scudder Elementary, an air of excitement prevailed. Any pretense of academics was just that. The children were too excited at the prospect of early dismissal, the icicles growing on the eaves, the possibility of snow, to concentrate on school books. The office was spinning with parents looking for children, children looking for parents, and staff that looked as if they wanted to fold their arms on their desks, put their heads down on their arms, and stay that way 'til the dream was over and the world had returned to normal.

I collected one child from Scudder, one from St. Stephen's Episcopal School, and two of my neighbors' children from Bowen Middle School, their parents being unable to reach the school in time from their out-of-town jobs. I dropped the children at the office and thought I would sneak out for a minute or two, run up to the grocery store, pick up a few items for the weekend.

The parking lot should have clued me in. I couldn't find a parking space, and as I stepped from my car, I heard familiar voices behind me—"Don't do it! Don't do it unless you're desperate!"

I turned to see two friends approaching, their arms laden with groceries, their faces haggard and bemused. The store, they said, was a zoo, a madhouse ... pick your cliché. You had to stand in line to get a shopping cart. People were stripping the shelves—no bread, no milk, no pinto beans, no chili meat. And then, when you finally filled your cart, you had to stand in a line that snaked down the aisles and around the back of the store. One man, in frustration, stood in line for twenty minutes, then finally shook his head and walked out, leaving his full grocery cart in line. Why go, they said, unless I was desperate.

I thought for a moment, surveyed the parking lot, and decided I wasn't even close to desperate.

My next stop was the video store. As I wedged my way through the door, past the lines of people, and looked at the empty shelves, I decided I wasn't desperate for videos, either. I headed back to the office, corralled the kids, and took them out for hot chocolate. Wimberley, it seemed, was outfitting its shared dream of winter.

Gradually, pieces of the town shut down. The Cypress Creek Cafe canceled much of the jazz festival scheduled for the weekend, because the musicians might not be able to make the drive from Austin. John Henry's Restaurant closed its doors, and the streets emptied of cars—or most of them.

Jitter's, the local gourmet coffee shop, experienced a boom in

business Friday morning as all the dedicated coffee drinkers—the ones who sit at the table for hours with their coffee, which is usually not gourmet—filtered in because their regular haunts were closed.

And the fun in Country Boys Grocery never stopped. Friday, says the manager, was almost as bad as Thursday. A kind of panic had set in when the weatherman mentioned sleet and freezing rain, and it didn't abate all weekend. The store ran out of bread, eggs, milk—all the basics—and sold more soup and chili fixings in two days than it usually sells in two weeks.

At one point, he said, there was a fifteen-minute wait for a basket. While every businessperson likes to see customers walk into the store, watching the food disappear from the shelves at the rate it was going was a little alarming. There was no way to replenish it.

And then, he said, the bread men didn't show up on Friday, because they were afraid of driving their trucks down the big hill. "We were breadless. I've never seen the bread guys not make it. They're like the post office. They're supposed to make it."

The manager says he and Shane, the produce manager, strolled into the parking lot Saturday morning to count the snowflakes. They counted seventy-three—the blizzard of '96.

He sees the panic as a kind of Texas thing. Mention ice or freeze, he says, and people assume the worst. They don't trust the weatherman. I could see his point. Ice up the roads and there's no telling what might happen. A good Texan is always prepared.

I was. I cooked fajitas Friday night for some clients—several of whom were from England. They were amazed, they said, that anyone would barbecue with icicles for a backdrop. They even took a picture. "This is Texas," I said. "We like our barbecue, and the weather could change in the next ten minutes." But I have to admit—it was kind of cold.

My children loved it. At one point, after turning my back for five minutes, I caught my youngest outside, barefoot, dressed only in a long t-shirt, breaking icicles off the railings. He wasn't cold, he said, and protested mightily against my insistence that he dress more appropriately.

But the older one caught on quickly. He pulled on five layers of clothes and grew rounder and less defined with each layer. If he could have made it to the grocery store, he probably would have wiped out whole shelves by himself in preparation for the cold. He was angry that I had not bought him gloves this winter, and that the only hats he could find didn't cover his ears.

The boys reveled in the outside, an unbridled energy propelling them through the weekend. "This isn't bad weather," was the oldest boy's refrain as he pedaled like a madman down the street on his bike. "This is *great* weather!"

I had to smile. They had too much energy to get cold. The kind of days that were shutting so many of us in were days they'd kill for in the north. Balmy. Temperate. Good-weather days.

I breathed in the cold air, wrapped myself in a long coat, and welcomed the change. I knew it would be brief—just long enough to keep the good dreams of winter alive. Just short enough to hold the bad dreams of winter at bay.

Circus

Circus day started early. Any day that involves an extra step in the going-to-school process starts early. Too early. And here we were, Cameron and I, trying to get ready to go to the circus.

It was a big event for both of us. For Cameron, it was the first outing his first-grade class had taken, and, reality aside, the word *circus* connotes magic to any child. *Circus* holds a world of possibility in its two short syllables. *Circus* is adrenaline and big animals and impossible stunts. *Circus* is a break from routine.

For me, *circus* meant a long, loud bus ride, three to a seat, into northeast Austin. It meant a hastily constructed tuna fish sandwich, dubious bananas, and a Powerade, something I never drink at home.

So why go when I didn't have to? When I could have pleaded too much work, not enough time, the demands of two careers? Why go when I had to put off people who needed to talk with me, people who were working for me, and myself, who was fighting a time crunch in my very bones? When I had to tell them all I was not available because I was going to the circus. Why go?

Because who would miss a circus? Who, given the opportunity, would miss seeing their child so excited he could talk of nothing else—so excited he actually raced through the morning procedure of waking and dressing and eating and hunting down shoes? I wouldn't miss it for anything.

So Cameron and I went to the circus. Everything else took a back seat. I got up extra early and made lists for the part of my life I was leaving behind. I made tuna fish sandwiches because that was what was in the pantry. I found two bananas and hoped the whole mess would survive the bus trip to Austin. We stopped at the grocery store and bought huge sports drinks and Nutter Butters, and we made it to school just in time not to be tardy, a condition I often find myself in. As we walked inside, Cameron hugged me and thanked me for getting him there on time.

Outside the school, the Shriners, who sponsor the trip to the Shrine Circus every year for Wimberley's first-graders, were waiting in their tall maroon fezzes.

"What are *those?*" Cameron asked, pointing to the fezzes.

"They're hats," I said.

"I've never seen a hat that looked like that," he said.

"Well, trust me," I said. "They're hats. Very special hats."

"Oh."

Each parent who chose to attend the circus was assigned two children. I had Cameron and Travis, who was quiet and held my hand tightly, entrusting me with his lunch box and his life. I was touched. Cameron, boisterous and high-spirited, red-headed and exuberant, tugged at the other child to join the party. Travis, a subdued redhead, if there is such a thing, was politely reticent. I wondered if the teacher, Mrs. Ingle, wasn't trying to balance the energies I would have to contend with.

Mr. Shirley was our bus driver. A tall grandfather of a man with a saving sense of humor and grandchildren of his own to sustain it, he warned us of safety rules, pointing out exits and exiting procedures. All would be well, he assured us, unless a 747 dropped out of the sky on top of us, in which case there was no exit.

"If that happened," said Cameron, "he wouldn't be able to drive the bus, would he?"

"Right," I said, "but that's not going to happen."

"How do you know?"

"I don't."

"Then why did you say that?"

"Never mind."

In the very front of the bus rode Harvey Aaron and his wife,

Pat. Harvey, who sat on an upside-down bucket, is Shrine president this year, and with his wide Mississippi drawl and wider smile, he seemed as excited about the circus as the children. But I know Harvey. I know what Harvey loves is being able to take the children to the circus. I think Harvey would do anything he could to make a child happy.

One thing he did was pass his fez around. I wasn't kidding when I told Cameron those fezzes were special hats, and I was a little uneasy about seeing the tall maroon hat with the rhinestone insignias on it and the long gold tassel get handed from child to child and tried on by half the bus, but Harvey didn't seem to be.

When we reached Buda, Travis tapped me on the shoulder.

"Are we there yet?" he asked in his polite, soft voice.

"No," I answered. "We're in Buda."

"Buda?" he said. "Where's Buda?"

"Right here."

"Oh."

Cameron, bored by the ride, managed to sit on my lap a good portion of the way, which had its moments. I miss holding my boys on my lap. Somehow, in the process of growing up, they got bigger. I don't really know when it happened, and I still pick up Cameron on occasion, but Malone, my older son, is beyond the picking-up stage, and Cameron is rapidly growing past the lap stage. He doesn't know that, though, and he wiggles a lot. Still, the bus ride had a ways to go, and my job, as I saw it, was to keep the peace, so I held him and rubbed my cheek against his red curls. He wiggled.

Mr. Shirley drove that bus with aplomb. We were the lead bus, and he took us on a tour of the Motorola and Tracor plants on the way. I didn't remember the plants from the same trip I had made three years earlier with my older son and thought maybe they had moved the site of the circus, but the truth was, Mr. Shirley wanted the children to get a good look at the site of Austin's leading industry, an educational detour, as it were. The other buses dutifully followed, and as we found the exit for 183, he called back to me, "Why didn't you tell me we were going the wrong way?"

"Yeah, Mom," said Cameron. "How come?"

The Travis County Expo Center is in the flatlands, in the middle of nowhere, an expansive compound of buildings that was surrounded that day by school buses and lines of children. We climbed off the bus, lunches in hand, and headed up the bleachers to our seats. The children were excited.

"Hey!" said one little girl, "It smells like my gerbil in here."

"That's elephant poop!" someone else announced. Through the doors in the arena at the far end we could see the big creatures moving like lumbering shadows, and the excitement mounted.

"When's it gonna start?" the children asked, the question running like a loose refrain up and down the bleachers.

"Soon," the parents answered, fiddling with drinks and lunch bags, encouraging children to use the restrooms before the show began, and climbing over legs and lunches on the way out.

The Shriners were everywhere. Visible in their fezzes, they helped direct parents and children, checked on the boys' restroom, when the moms had been standing outside for a while, and generally kept an eye on things.

When the lights lowered, a spontaneous rush of applause broke from the schoolchildren, who came from all over the Austin area, a release of the anticipation. Cameron leaned forward and stuck his thumb in his mouth, a tactic he resorts to in moments of excitement or extreme concentration.

And then the motorcycle guy came out. In the middle of the arena, they had set a huge oval, metal cage that he rode in as if it were an open highway, executing loops and circles that seemed impossible and breathtakingly dangerous. Cameron breathed beside me in amazement.

"Oh, Mom," he said, "you were right. This was worth it to get here."

Behind us, another little boy sighed, "Dude, it'd be cool if I knew how to do that!"

Acrobats followed, their sleek bodies glittering in white sequins.

"Ooooh," sighed another little boy as the woman swung through the air, her long black hair flying behind her, "Ooooh, she's so pretty."

When the Star Wars theme hit the loudspeakers, the children all knew the tune. Recognition in a world of strangeness is always welcome.

The big cats amazed the children with their surly grace, and the clowns incited the crowd to yelling matches so loud that Cameron covered his ears. When one of the acrobats performed her act through the air, held aloft by a rope of her hair, a little girl who had been crying earlier as her mother brushed the tangles from her long hair, scoffed, "Nawww, that'd be easy. That wouldn't hurt."

The children were entranced by the six-year-old contortionist who could bend her body like rubber, by the ponderous dance of the elephants, by the grown-up boy on the little bitty bike who could do all the tricks they practice on their bikes in the driveway.

Lunchtime was a mess of junk food—of Lunchables and sports drinks, of sodas and chips and cookies and things you would never eat at home. We ate too many Nutter Butters and made our way through soggy tuna sandwiches, the smell of which took me immediately back to my childhood lunch box. Cameron spilled tuna fish down the front of my shirt while attempting to free his lettuce from the confines of his sandwich because he doesn't believe that salads belong on sandwiches, but he knew I did and thought he'd give his lettuce to me.

By the time the circus returned to the tightrope act, I smelled like the lunch box, and when the child in front of me knocked his soda over on top of my feet and lunch bag, I was ready to throw the whole mess away, but I couldn't. We still had Nutter Butters left.

The kids had the tightrope act all figured out. It was a magic rope. The acrobat could ride a bike on it because the wheels had no tires.

"Do you think you could do that on a bike with no tires?" I asked Cameron.

"No," he said. "I don't have enough balance in me."

"Me neither," I said, feeling it strongly. "Me neither."

"This is real," said one boy in a voice of hushed awe. "This is like TV, but this is real."

I was pleased to see that the ubiquitous blur of the TV had not erased the capacity for amazement in the real world.

The final act was a human cannonball, and I found myself lost in daydream as they readied the stuntman for the big blast. When they shot him out of the cannon, it took me by surprise, and I jumped.

"Wow!" said Cameron. "That was so loud it hurt my feet!"

A child in the back cried, so concerned was he with the safety of the stuntman. I wanted to tell him it was just a circus, and then I reminded myself that it was real. That is what made it so special. It was very real.

The bus ride on the way back seemed longer, hotter, and louder than the first half of the trip. Travis wilted in the sunlight against the window until I picked him up and set him in my lap with my back as a sunguard. He shared my sports drink and watched in amazement as Cameron and a friend across the aisle poked and prodded each other all the way home. I shouted a conversation across the seat with a friend and weathered the hot air blowing through the open window.

Arriving back at Scudder, hoarse and windblown and pummeled, I decided I was the one who had been shot from the cannon.

But the children had stars in their eyes still and talked about the elephants, the beautiful women, the motorcycle guy. They were still puzzling on the possibilities the world has to offer, the glamour and the silliness.

And that is why I go to the circus now—to watch my children. The Shriners may have thought they were providing an opportunity for our children, and they were, but they also provided me with an opportunity, and I owe them my thanks. I loved the circus I got to see, the bright lights in the eyes, the reinterpretation of the world. To me, the children are the amazing possibilities, and their awe and laughter is a fine, breezy tightrope act I would travel any length to watch.

Thanksgiving

I looked up last week and noticed we'd used up all the sparklers from the Fourth of July. The back-to-school clothes bought in September had holes in the knees, and Cameron had already consigned his latest pair of shoes to that black hole that claims so much of his footwear. The Halloween candy was gone; no one had put on a costume in weeks; and the Veterans Day poppy had fallen off my coat.

Outside the window, the cypress trees had rusted bare, sifted their dry feathers down to the surface of the creek where they gathered in still pools of winter water. I scraped ice off my car window the other morning. The phone is ringing with questions about cooking Thanksgiving dinner.

Is it Thanksgiving already, and when did it come? I guess if you're a passenger in a car and so busy looking at the road map that you never look outside the window, you can chart the course and never see the passage.

The world has a way of overwhelming us these days. Life seems to run at a speed hinging on the progress of technology, and we discard what takes a second too long to process. In between trying to catch our breath before we hit the next curve and trying to maneuver the road in the highest of style, we feel our own inadequacies. The human soul can only run so far at the speed of megabytes and electronic impulses. We are pushing ourselves so hard and so fast that we may miss the sensation of freefall at the end of the cliff, discovering that we overran the edge only when we hit the bottom.

So today I'm going to look up for a moment, catch the patchy blue overhead, listen to the quiet. I'm going to reflect on the moments lived to a slower music, on the flavors held in the mouth long enough to remember, on the steady heartbeat of good and lasting memories. In a fragmented world, it is that slow steadiness that will finally keep us alive and wanting to be there.

I am going to string those moments like melting moons of freshwater pearls on a necklace, and I am going to wear them for Thanksgiving.

Last summer, toward the end of the heat and the beginning of school, we decided if we were going to take a vacation, we had better do it. With time and money constraints, we decided to spend the weekend before school started on the beach on Padre Island. We would camp out the first night and find a hotel room and pool the second night.

"Whoaaaa," said my friends with the kind of laugh that makes you think that what you're about to embark on isn't funny. "Whoaaah. Have you ever spent the night on the beach? With children?

"Have you ever cooked on the beach? How do you feel about sand? In your teeth?"

We took a tent. With small boys as part of the scheme, you have to take a tent. But growing up on camping trips in the Sierras of northern California, I never slept in tents, so I wasn't concerned by the logistics that reasoned that five people would not fit comfortably in a small tent.

We arrived near dark, so the tent was erected by feel and guess and general goodwill. The boys spread their bags on the nylon floor and played games with their flashlights, creating monster shadows on the sides until we threatened something vague and unlikely and they grew quiet and pretended to sleep

Jimmy and I looked at each other. Somehow the towering canopies of redwoods in the Sierras had created more of a shelter than the open sky of the Texas coastline.

"Let's sleep in the van," said Jimmy, heading back up the dune.

"No way," I said. "I came to sleep on the beach."

"But there's wind, and there's sand, and ..."

"It's just sand," I said, but I wanted to add something about the vastness. I wanted to say, "But it's just so open."

I didn't, though. I had come to sleep on the beach, so we unrolled the foam pad and sheets and pillow and lay down beneath more light than I had ever known existed. It was starlight as far as we could see and farther. It unrolled beyond the stretches of our imagination. It shimmied on the waves and pulsed a steady brightness. It breathed and sang a silence unparalleled by any music. I think I fell asleep and woke a dozen times that night, my heart always expanding to take in the night.

The inhabitants of the tent, like natives of a foreign land, had finally fallen asleep, and the tent loomed motionless in the starlight. I knew they were dreaming in a privacy no one could touch, and I lay still in my own timeless isolation and listened to the constancy of the waves breaking on the dark sand, like a promise of forever in a world tripping over the heels of its own change.

It was a night cast in silver, immutable and luminous. When the daylight finally tipped the balance of the dark, the water claimed the light. A few people walked the early beach in search of shells or solitude, but I lay back and watched the starlight fade until it was just iridescence in the sky, and I will never forget that night. It's a promise I hear again and again, and I know I can always go back. The music of the stillness will always play somewhere.

I have a recipe file that has become something of a joke in my kitchen. Written on index cards and stuffed inside a box, the best, most-used recipes are almost illegible at this point. Weathered through use and spillage, through wet hands and hurried hands, they are out of order and must be riffled through frequently to find the errant measurements for Southwestern Cheesecake, or Jonnie's Rolls, or Mom's Carrot Cake.

When they don't show up on the first perusal, I chide myself for my disorganization, so flagrant it seems willful at times. I tell myself I have made the dish so many times I shouldn't need the recipe. I fume and fear at loss of something treasured. So I have started sharing the recipes with people I trust to love them as well as I do. Then, when I can't find them, I know who to call, counting on the world to keep a better card file than the one I store in my kitchen.

But usually the recipes show up. They had just been tucked under the wrong heading, and since the headings on the divider cards have faded, no one knows the system but me, and that can be frightening at times. But for all the chaos associated with that file box, I love it. It has become the receptacle of more than recipes. It has become the arbor of memories.

I can pull out the yeast roll recipe and think of the friend who gave it to me, asking only that I give her credit when they came out good. The rolls are fluffy like the pillows dreams are made of, and they taste faintly sweet and wondrously buttery. Jonnie Stansbury of Blair House took me into her kitchen and walked me through them the first time. Covered with flour, she patted the very soft dough and told me to treat it as I would a lover, treat it with a feather touch. Otherwise, she cautioned, the dough will toughen and turn on you, like a lover spurned.

I have made many of those rolls, too many to count. I have run out of them at feasts because they were so good, and I have found that when I rush them, they are never as good. I have determined that only one in love with the grace of good food can make them the way they're supposed to be made.

Another recipe is so dog-eared, the yellow card has more the texture of soft doeskin than paper. It holds the ingredients for a carrot cake that will make you cry When other people brag on their carrot cakes, I smile inside. I am not, by nature, a competitive person, but I know I have the best. I don't tell them, though. I just bake up a pan of the dark, rich cake, studded in raisins and pecans and the round, deep baritone of the cinnamon voice. I smooth it with cream cheese and butter and snowdrifts of powdered sugar, and I watch their eyes widen in disbelief.

"Where," they stumble, "where did you find this piece of heaven?"

"My mother gave it to me," I always say, and she did. She and my father gave me the great love of food that allows the stroke of a lover when the world is too hurried. They taught me to search out the unusual, to take the time to savor it, to collect the recipes that build the foundations for the emerging dreams.

Cooking can be hurried. It often is when it becomes a business, but it also teaches the value of a loving pace. That which is tended as if it matters has a better chance of turning out right than food that is thrown in the pot without the memories attached. The disorganization of my card file may serve to slow me down just enough to remember the taste of the foods I have grown to love, the memories I have chosen to keep.

I have two boys and a sweetheart who run through my life with a masculine gusto that prompts me to yell, "Take it out of the kitchen!" on a frequent basis. They are loud, and at least two of them are getting bigger every day. They leave their toys on the floor and their clothes in the bathroom, and they talk in foreign accents that suggest multiple personalities. Even the youngest has discovered his Irish roots and a gift of mimicry that makes my house sound like the United Nations on Cultural Diversity Day.

But they have taught me well the value of taking time. Rushing the three men in my life results in a tough dough. Sometimes it is inevitable. Always it is frustrating. I find that if I back away and reenter the room slowly, they will listen, and, better yet, I will hear. They will put their arms around my neck. They will tell me they love me.

And I believe in that promise of forever in this world of disposable change.

Those are the moments best slowed to still frames. Those are the moments left to believe in.

This Thanksgiving will have its share of disorganization leading up to the turkey on the table. I know it will. In my life, there is no other way. People will wander through the juggling act of the kitchen and say, "How do you do it?"

I will adjust my pearl necklace and say, "You don't want to know."

143

But in the end we will sit down together. The youngest will sing a blessing in his pure voice, with or without an Irish accent. The oldest will eat more rolls than turkey. Maybe we will serve a carrot cake. I will hold the hand of the man I love, and outside, the stars will gather at the windows.

We will have leftovers for days. We will all slow down. We will remember to remember. And we will give thanks for the memories, for the promises of forever.

Christmas Travel

We had it all planned, the escape from life as we knew it: We would cook like crazy right up until Christmas. We would fashion steamed Christmas puddings from persimmons and cinnamon, plump raisins, and rum and them swim the whole thing in lemon sauce. We would swirl dizzy dances of mashed sweet potatoes and buttery russets. We would pull puffed golden corn puddings from the oven and set them beside spinach madeleines. Hams would float in cloves and apricots and bourbon.

We would meet all our catering needs on schedule, the kitchen redolent with the spicy fragrance of Christmas. We would meet them with ease and forethought and a minimum of rushing.

And while we were cooking, we would buy Christmas presents — an electric train that we expected to be demolished by Valentine's Day for the train man, a remote-control car for the teenager, watercolor pencils for the budding artist, *The Collected Works of William Butler Yeats* for the poet, a contribution toward driver's ed for the aspiring driver, candy, earrings, music, metal detectors, popcorn, books . . .

We would buy and put up the tree, decorate the railing, string the outside of the house in lights, and sing Christmas carols through the season. We would cater for parties and go to parties as guests.

We would make airplane reservations for Christmas Day and celebrate with the family staying behind on Christmas Eve, when we would hold a glorious Christmas celebration burnished in candlelight and fine food and the frivolous formality of Christmas paper strewn across the living room floor like a seasonal shedding of skin.

We would arrange to have the pets fed and the business running while we were gone. We would leave phone numbers and keys and lists and goodwill in our wake. We would do it all better than our mothers and the magazine doyennes. And then we would be out of here.

I love the season. I truly do, but I approach it each year with trepidation, fearful of the crunch, the last-minute phone calls that I can't and won't turn down. I make more lists than I make the entire balance of the year and lose most of them. I wander through the stores distracted by the abundance of celebration, by the dreams of the season. I listen to my children's wish list grow and grow to the point that they can't remember what's on it, and I despair of meeting their bright eyes in a reasonable fashion.

This year, we decided to go away after Christmas, to escape the reminders of a season so dizzy and dense it holds the blur of a green-and-red Ferris wheel in retrospect. We decided to visit family in California. We would leave Christmas Day and return New Year's Day for a decided discount on fares and a sense of adventure. We would arrange our time strategically in the weeks preceding, and all would go without a hitch. That was the plan.

We bought the Christmas tree early and strung it with more lights than the heavens provide. Although there was some commiseration among the members of the Christmas tree committee about why we weren't buying the $85 noble pine or the $95 blue spruce, we came home with a lovely tree, a semisymmetrical Douglas fir that suited our purposes very well. At least some of us thought so.

The lights were breathtaking, and even before we gilded the tree with all of the thousands of ornaments collected over the years, I loved nothing more than to plug it in early in the mornings when I first walked through the quiet, cold house. It lit the breaking day like falling stars, like fireworks frozen for a moment in the winter dawn.

When it was almost completed — ornaments weighing down the boughs — the boys came into the kitchen one morning before school and said, "Mom, what happened to the lights on the Christmas tree?"

Most of them had gone out. In the midst of making bread, I pulled my hair with my floured hands, as if that would help, and turned to Jimmy, who had strung the tree with lights.

He shrugged. "Must be a bad light in there somewhere," he said.

So Jimmy and his son revisited the strands of lights tangled like crazed back roads through the tree and fixed the problem. The next time it happened, a week or two later, we bought new lights and circumvented the lifeless one, creating an infrastructure of wire and bulbs with which we are still dealing.

Currently, we are arguing over whether to salvage any of the strands or to throw them all away and start over next year, and I have developed a whole new philosophy on capitalism and greed based on the fallibility of Christmas lights. I mean, if we can put a man on the moon ...

"Greed," says Jimmy. "Greed."

So we cooked our way through most of December and did our Christmas shopping two days before the actual day, which was, by some people's standards, early and teetering on the edge of compulsion. We have other friends who buy and wrap their presents weeks and months ahead of time, but we don't understand that concept. It is not a part of our abstract thinking.

True to form, we wrapped the presents Christmas Eve day, and then only because we were opening them that night.

The family all showed up, and friends dropped by during the day to sip on wine and Irish creme. I cooked all day for the last-minute jobs, then cooked our dinner, which we ate fashionably late because it wasn't ready earlier.

The children clamored at my elbows all day.

"Just one present, please? Just one now and the rest later?"

"No!"

"Then will you open one of yours?"

"No!"

"Why not?"

Children don't understand the benefits of anticipation, and they probably never will.

The last clients picked up their Christmas food at 11 P.M., on their way home from the airport, and we were in bed by 2 A.M., primed to rise early, pack our bags, write last-minute notes, and fly over the snow-crusted mountains to California, sipping Chardonnay all the way, while the children played quietly in the seats beside us with their new Christmas toys.

It happened like this.

We arose early, and I began packing. Jimmy cleared the living room floor of the Christmas Eve wreckage. I scrounged through the mound of clean clothes on top of the dryer for Cameron's socks and underwear, which fall through some designated black hole with alarming regularity. I had even bought him a new bag of socks, anticipating the problem, but those, too, were gone.

With two pairs in hand and one on his feet, I consoled myself that they sold socks in California, if it came to that, and finished their packing in less than an hour and a half, leaving their suitcase on the sofa for a few last-minute additions still in the dryer. In the meantime, seven-year-old Cameron lay on the floor and cried because it wasn't snowing and it was Christmas.

"It never snows here on Christmas," I said.

"Well, it did last year," he said.

"No, it didn't. This is Texas you live in. Central Texas. It doesn't snow on Christmas."

"Why do we have to live in Texas?" Followed by a long wail.

I packed my own bag in considerably less time, and we bundled still-damp clothes from the dryer into a garbage bag and stuffed them into Jimmy's suitcase, which had more space because he is a man. We mounded the eclectic and aging baggage in the dining room and proceeded to load it into the tiny rent car we were using because we had hit a deer in the van and were having it repaired while we were gone.

I left stacks of notes behind for my catering staff and rearranged a refrigerator so that everything would be easy to find. I mentally counted the keys I had distributed and placed one in a strategic location known only to half of Wimberley in case someone forgot their key or needed to get in the house and didn't have one.

I debated whether to haul the large and venerable dog outside, the dog who has learned well the meaning of suitcases and wouldn't even look at us when we left. He had wrapped himself on his cushion into as tight a ball as a 100-pound dog can manage, and he was sulking. I loved on him, told him we would be back, and decided to leave him inside, knowing the neighbors would check on him later in the day. They had a key and were feeding him. He ignored me.

We piled into the car, a large suitcase wedged between the two boys in the back seat, delivered a last-minute persimmon pudding to an ailing friend, and headed for the airport. On time.

"This is amazing," I said. "We need to pat ourselves on the back. We actually pulled this whole thing off. We met our obligations. We had our family Christmas. We left all necessary communications and keys where we were supposed to leave them. We packed. And we're going to get there in time. I'm so proud of us!"

Malone and Cameron, who had resigned himself to a less than white Christmas, and Jimmy, who was driving, and I, who was starting to breathe normally again—we all clapped and patted ourselves and arrived at the airport and unloaded the car and discovered that I had left the boy's suitcase with an entire week's worth of clothes in it sitting on the sofa at the house.

"Let's just get on the plane," I said. "We'll figure something out. We're *not* going back."

My voice, which moments earlier had been draped in the soft silks of leisure and relief, was edged to a fine blade of steel. The boys knew the tone. They eyed each other in some sort of rare brotherly agreement and closed down the impending wail.

As Jimmy disappeared with the car to the remote parking lot and I herded the boys into the airport toward the departure gate, I sensed that we had patted ourselves too soon on the back.

Sure enough, Jimmy surfaced at the gate with the news that every parking lot in the airport was full, except for the valet parking lot, which costs something just this side of a daily fortune, so he left the car there, and I found out that the airlines will not ship bags that are not accompanied by a passenger without charging another fortune, so I could not have the boys' suitcase sent later.

We both looked at each other with the blank stares that offer no solution and herded the boys onto the plane. The flight attendant took one look at us and offered us free drinks for Christmas. On the second leg of the journey, the attendant brought us complimentary champagne. I closed my eyes and tried to sleep, thinking I would deal with the world when we arrived in California, but there the plot only thickened.

As we unloaded the car in the driveway, my brother came out to tell us that the neighbor had called to tell us that the key we had given her wouldn't open the door. The dog, who had vomited all over the floor, was inside dancing a jig, and they couldn't find the key I had strategically hidden. Also, the Christmas pork roast wasn't cooking fast enough. My mother couldn't find her persimmon pudding recipe. And what were we supposed to do next?

I called the neighbor, who had removed a window from the house and opened the door to free the dog, delaying her Christmas dinner in the process. I retrieved the missing recipe from my card file of recipes, which I had brought with me, and I turned the heat up on the pork. We decided to buy the boys a couple of changes of sweatsuits and leave the car in valet parking. We plowed through the roller coaster in Santa Cruz, the tech museum in San Jose, and the Golden Gate Bridge in San Francisco, through Dungeness crabs, sushi, Chinese food, and a sunrise on a northern coastline on New Year's Day. We wedged ourselves back into a tiny rent car with more luggage than we had left with and weathered the trip back to Austin, at which point Malone caught the flu. As we stopped at the last fast-food restaurant open on the way to Wimberley and unfolded the boys from the back of the car, Cameron asked if we should pat ourselves on the back.

I looked at the next 364 days sprawled in front of us like a litter of unmanageable pups, and I said —

"No. No, boys. Not yet."

 Christmas

"I saw your tree," my youngest son said to his friend's grandfather. "It's not very good, is it?"

The grandfather took this in graciously and said, "Well, Cameron, you haven't seen it with decorations on it. It looks a lot better now. Come see."

So Cameron obliged, and after gazing for a moment at the shimmering creation of Christmas lights and ornaments, he conceded that it did look a lot better.

"But," he said. "It's not as good as my mom's tree. My mom has the best tree in the world."

That has made it all worthwhile.

Putting up a tree is a ritual most families go through about this time every year. Some, because of allergies, expense, convenience, or environmental concerns, have opted for artificial trees, but even those families cannot escape their tryst with the tree. They still must dig it out of the attic, fluff its mashed branches, then assemble limb by limb the ersatz evergreen.

And once it is standing, they must still untangle the lights and unwrap the shiny glass globes, the tiny Santas, last year's crumpled ribbons. There's virtually no escape.

I like the real trees. I like the way they smell—the coolness that drifts from their branches like some snow-laden mountain breath. They smell of greenness, of winter, of Christmas.

So this year, I set out with the boys and a friend to pick out a tree. We went early, the week after Thanksgiving, knowing if we waited we would not get a tree. Life was getting too busy, pushing day after day behind it until I could see Christmas slipping by without a tree.

And, as it turns out, that was a good decision. This year, it seems, if you didn't get your tree early, chances are you got a brown tree, or a deformed tree, or a tree that was not the height of your choosing.

But we got a pretty good tree. We drove around the different tree lots and pondered Douglas firs, noble pines, Texas pines. We asked the treemen to stand the trees up for us, twirl them around. We fingered the needles to determine freshness and breathed the deep green air of Christmas.

Finally we found one that suited our tastes—a noble pine, tall, full, and somewhat symmetrical. We watched the tree man swath it in plastic and shove it into the back of the van. All the way home, we breathed its scent.

Night had settled in when we arrived home, so we pulled the tree out of the van and left it on the front porch 'til the next day. The boys wanted to put it up immediately, but I was too tired from the tree search to contemplate dragging it through the kitchen to the living room and facing the trail of needles it invariably leaves.

The next day was warmer than December should be, and as I stood outside grilling asparagus on the barbecue pit, I glanced over at the tree and noticed that moisture had collected on the plastic where the sun was beating down on it, and our beautiful green tree was mellowing to a golden brown.

Panic-stricken, I ripped the plastic from the tree, implored a friend to cut the base, and wedged it into a bucket of water. Fortunately, the brown was in the area we decided should face the wall.

Next came the task of setting it up. In past years, coaxing the tree into its stand had been a task that caused family wars. But this year, I had decided it would be easy—as if mere deciding could make it happen.

The first go-round *was* easy. My friend stuck around to help, and the tree settled into the broad plastic stand with grace and goodwill. It even obliged us by standing up straight the first

time. All was well until I added water to the stand and noticed, just before I began to string the lights, that water seemed to be seeping from the tree stand and pooling on the wooden floor.

The tree stand, it appeared, had a leak in it. At that point, my friend remembered something pressing he had to do and left, which was just as well, because I could see that setting the tree up was not going to be quite as easy as I thought.

I took a deep breath, unscrewed the tree from the stand, and headed over to the store to pick up a new stand.

Back at the house with the new metal stand, I sat down by the tree to read the instructions, something I don't do well, not easily given to following other people's dreams of sequence.

Maria, a friend who had been standing back watching the tree-raising with barely concealed amusement, offered to help. So together, fierce with pride that we, as women, could make this tree go up and go up straight, we put the tree up.

I wish I had a video of the event. We could have won awards, Maria and I, wrestling with that tree until the skin on my hands was raw and I wanted to cry but couldn't for laughing. At one point, I remember lying on my back with the tree looming over me, and Maria on the other end trying to keep it from crushing me. It was as if that pine had a mind of its own and refused to be screwed to a stand.

It soon became evident that the metal stand was an illogical, poorly conceived device, and although the box it came in clearly said the stand would support an eight-foot tree, it would not. Perhaps its inventors had not dreamed of an eight-foot tree of this majesty, this breadth, this willfulness.

After pushing the tree into an upright position, we noticed that the stand was wobbling on the floor and the tree was listing dangerously to the right. Seconds after we noticed, as if to prove a point, the tree fell over.

So we started again. Maria carefully inspected the first stand and decided I had put too much water in it, which had leaked out the screw holes. For lack of a better solution, we decided to try again, and the third time was the charm. The tree gave in, straightened up, and finally stood like a Christmas tree is supposed to, allowing me to drape tiny lights over its branches and dazzle its limbs with probably the most eclectic collection of ornaments in town.

I like the incandescence of white lights, but Christmas is a time of sharing, and, at my children's insistence, I interwove my white lights with their colored lights, cursing the devilish mind that invented the system that empowers those tiny bulbs.

(You know, when one bulb burns out or shakes a little loose in its socket, half the strand goes, and you spend the next hour or two trying to find the troublemaker, all the while promising yourself you will just buy new lights next year — they're cheap enough — and this won't happen again. But it does. It always happens. It's part of Christmas.)

My children wanted to help decorate, which is why I have invested heavily in the shiny glass balls that go on sale every year during the season. They broke more than several in their zeal but carried on undeterred. When they had decorated enough to lose interest, I took over, filling in what they had not decorated, which was more than half the tree, most of it in the upper reaches.

But we finished, finally, and they stood in awe at the sparkling creation we had wrought. I, too, felt a little of their awe, as if this tree had unsevered roots that connected it to all the trees of my past — the elegant, understated blue spruces of my childhood, the cedars I tried for a few years before deciding they were not true Christmas trees, the trees we cut in the Santa Cruz mountains, the bushy Texas pines we pulled from local lots.

I think this tree shares my memories — of holding my oldest son one year beside its branches, watching him finger my new necklace made of folk charms and trinkets.

"Look, Mom," he said, "it's the baby Jesus."

In his hand, he held a tiny watermelon charm. The baby Jesus?

"Yes," he said. "Jesus in a watermelon suit."

Of my younger brother, when he was a boy, making everyone gather around the tree after the decorating while he carried in milk and cookies from the kitchen, insisting that we eat, drink, and sing Christmas carols around its lights.

Of the nights last year when my overhead lights burned out,

and my life was lit by the magic of the tree, a warm light, not to read by, but to dream by. When I finally took the tree down, I had to find someone with a long enough ladder to change out the bulbs.

Of my youngest son standing before that glowing green, the lights mirrored and flashing in his eyes, his head tilted back, smiling.

"Mom," he will say again and again. "Mom," I will hear every Christmas. "That's the most beautiful tree in the world."

Gifts

In a frenzy of giving, shoppers crowded the stores, swarmed the highways, tore yard after yard of wrapping paper and tape from their rolls. I saw them, was, in fact, part of them, grew dizzy in the mob and numb from the barrage of the season.

Living here has spoiled me. I pull away from crowds, maneuver urban streets with a timidity that brands me as a tourist, an out-of-towner, at best. But I braved them all last month for the sake of the season. I had to buy supplies for my catering business, toys for my children.

Over the years—perhaps because of circumstance, perhaps because of inclination—I have become a less than avid shopper. I make routine rounds to certain stores and force myself into others when necessity demands. This year, I managed to avoid Toys "R" Us but toured the aisles of Wal-Mart and Target, trying to talk my brain into shifting gears, into thinking like a five-year-old or an eight-year-old boy.

As the gears began their shift, I realized the problem. Five- and eight-year-old boys want everything. There is no limit to their desires when it comes to acquiring things—toys, candy, books, toys, sporting goods, electronic games, toys ... toys ... toys. ...

I shifted back to thinking like the mother of two small boys who is trying to shop in their best interest, ensuring their satisfaction while maintaining her own sanity and sense of decency.

I returned home from these expeditions with my arms os-

156

tensibly laden with bags of cranberries, exotic mushrooms, pork tenders, smelly French cheeses, prosciutto, persimmons. The usual for the season. The kind of stuff that makes my children turn up their noses in disgust and back away from the car. The kind of things that make my youngest child draw a picture of the family, all of us in portrait stiffness, except for me, Mom, my arm outstretched with a rectangle dangling from it. Underneath it, he has written, "Mom with a grocery bag." My usual attire.

What they didn't know was that beneath the crab meat and kalamata olives, sandwiched between the baguettes and the brown sugar was a three-foot-long remote-control firetruck, a Caterpillar-type vehicle that will roll over anyone's foot, a microscope with a viewing screen, a small Instamatic camera, several candy canes. ...

What I forgot in the dizziness of shopping was that almost everything, with the exception of the candy canes, required batteries. I remembered that at 2 A.M. Christmas morning, which is when I finished wrapping presents.

Christmas is hard on children. I remember the interminability of the wait. When five-year-old Cameron wailed that it was too long to wait, that ten days was too long, that five days was too long, that he'd never make it through Christmas Eve, the words danced in my head like a long-forgotten song that surfaces when the first few chords are played on the car radio.

He did actually see one of the gifts, but assured me with great sincerity that he would forget what it was before Christmas, since Christmas was so far away.

Eight-year-old Malone was a little more tolerant of the wait, although I wouldn't call him patient. He had already debunked the Santa myth and chose only to believe when he thought it would aggravate me, having already done so through his disbelief.

But they waited, as we all did, because I made them wait. I did not have time to wrap the presents before that edge between Christmas Eve and Christmas morning. I never do. It's part of the tradition. None of this leisurely tying of exotic bows and thoughtful gift-wrap choices for me. At midnight, the cutting and wrapping and taping begins with a vengeance that is only surpassed by the vengeance with which the gifts are unwrapped.

This year, like many in the past, I had a Christmas Eve party, an open house where friends dropped by for eggnog, tamales, chili, and whatever else sneaked out of the refrigerator while I wasn't thinking.

I spent a few days before the party cooking, decorating, and watching my home come together in a kind of Christmas fantasy painted in greens and reds, limned in gold. Even the boys joined in. Malone, the oldest, wrapped his small personal tree in a stranglehold of beads and lights, and tied silver ribbons on every available hook or drawer pull in his room. Cameron, the younger brother, trailed me around the house, begging for the gold glitter that fell from the dried baby's breath I had purchased in Austin. When I wasn't looking, he shook the flowers vigorously into his hair, emerging a glittering, grinning child with gilded red curls.

They accompanied me one cold afternoon on a search for chinaberries, which I dusted with gold spray paint. They didn't have much use for the withered ivory berries before I pulled out the spray paint, but when that gold showed up in a light iridescence along the limbs and berries, they were fascinated.

They didn't think much of my light-handed approach, however, and commandeered the paint can when I had finished to paint their own berries, which came out a solid, thick, drooping gold. In fact, a lot of things came out gold—rocks, wood chips, portions of the driveway.

That held their attention for a while, but the bare space under the tree worked like a magnet, and they, like the stray paper clips and nails a magnet collects, kept returning to it. Where were the presents? I hadn't wrapped them yet, I explained. Why not? I hadn't had time, I explained. Why not? I've been too busy working, shopping, cooking, cleaning. Silence, then—When *are* you going to wrap them?

I tried the Santa Claus thing—Christmas Eve, Santa's bag of toys, sleeping children—but they just scowled. It was one of the times Malone chose not to believe the myth, and Cameron sensed injustice in the world. His friends had presents under *their* trees, he said. Well, I said with great finality, we don't. Yet.

But we did, finally, thanks to a bunch of foolhardy friends who braved the eggnog and dishwashing to stay up with me and help wrap presents. It was wonderful and silly. I never knew an assembly line could be so much fun. When I couldn't find the boys' stockings, we resorted to individually wrapping the whoopee cushion, the bicycle horns, and the Silly Putty in an assortment of brightly colored socks. The twenty-five diecast cars went into a pair of boxer shorts printed with fish and tied with a bright, curled ribbon.

Christmas morning came early. It always does. It's part of the tradition. Paper flew, ribbons flew, the house became a repository for Christmas confetti. The boys were elated, amazed, inspired.

And it wasn't all take and no give on their part. Malone is old enough now to have discovered the joy of giving, and I opened a small box with a silver chain purchased at the PTO Christmas store, another box with a clock from the local hardware store, the obvious gift from a young man who wears a watch on each wrist and a stopwatch around his neck. Cameron received from him a Slinky and an airplane he had made from wood.

Cameron had given me a cutting board some days before — he couldn't wait for Christmas. He had made the board himself, nailed together two large trapezoidal shapes with impossible angles and proudly handed it to me, knowing he had given me something I could use. He asks me every day when I'm going to use it. I haven't told him I'm afraid to.

They were happy, once we bought all the batteries in the grocery store. They were pleased until they remembered the things on their list they hadn't found under the tree. Cameron, for example, felt shorted in the train department. He had wanted and expected a Christmas filled with nothing but train paraphernalia, having inherited the train gene from someone. And he did receive a few train-related gifts, but apparently not enough. Specifically, he did not receive the subway he had asked for, and I don't mean the sandwich. I told him I couldn't find one.

Malone realized at some point in the day, as he was constructing some intricate Lego fantasy, that he had not unwrapped an organizer, the kind that would hold all his important phone numbers and help him schedule his appointments.

The kind that would allow him to keep track of his gas mileage, his expense account, his life.

I have to admit that I found several organizers but balked at the idea of paying that much money for an eight-year-old to organize his life. The idea kind of scared me, too. I'm not so good at using one of those myself. Maybe I should give him mine, except he's already pointed out to me that the calendar is two years old and I'm not using the sections for the purposes they were intended. I told him I had looked for one and would keep looking.

They got over their disappointments, as children do on Christmas. The low is as important as the high. It helps to level things out so the child can finally lay himself flat on the floor and run the small cars under the furniture, direct the firetruck out the back door, compare his loot with the neighbor's.

All things considered, we didn't do badly at all. They're still playing with their toys, the batteries haven't run out yet, and I'm wearing a silver chain and still trying to figure out how to use the cutting board.

There was one item on Malone's Santa list that we haven't opened yet. In addition to asking for the Legos, the chapter books, the candy canes, and a pet iguana (which he also didn't get), he asked in his small, neat handwriting for a happy New Year.

I did, too. That's one long, bright ribbon we hope to unfurl.

Diet

The realization that we're growing older presents itself in many packages, and we begin to unwrap each year as if it were a Trojan horse — compelling on the outside, rife with enemy within.

I think the first clue that my body wasn't responding with the enthusiasm it once had came about eight years ago. I was trying to relax on a California beach with my family, all of us gathered to celebrate my brother's wedding. My youngest son was still an infant, bonneted against the sun, eating sand and miserable about the whole affair. My oldest son was three and intent on disrobing at every possible opportunity and throwing himself into the chilly waves of the Pacific Ocean.

I was torn between visiting with the family I seldom saw, wiping the baby's mouth free of sand and retying his hat to his small and very red head, and snatching my older son's swim trunks from the waves as I implored him to put them back on.

Relief came when the baby fell asleep beneath a makeshift tent of towels and the older one discovered the sand dunes. With his aunt, who cross-country skis and kayaks and hikes in the rivers and the mountains of Wyoming, he proceeded to wreak acrobatic havoc on the mountains of sand behind us.

I watched for a while as he raced up the sand to the top, then leaped into the air for the sand to catch him halfway down, as he somersaulted and cartwheeled and executed any number of other gymnastic feats I couldn't recognize down through the glistening, welcoming sands. Then I turned my attention back to my family and friends.

"Mom." I felt the tug at my elbow. "Mom, come somersault down the dunes with me."

Somersault down the dunes? I stared at him in disbelief. "You want me to somersault down the dunes?"

I thought about explaining how proud I was just to be able to fit back into a swimsuit after carrying his brother for nine months, about how I was thirty-five years old and hadn't somersaulted down anything in a very long time, about how I didn't really want to somersault down the dunes.

And then I thought, *Why not?* I used to love somersaults. I was never a gymnast, but I could always do a pretty fair somersault. In fact, as a child, I had somersaulted down many sand dunes and hills, and maybe I should give myself that opportunity again. You're only as old as you think you are. Or something like that.

So I followed him back to the soft, sloping dune and began the hike up through the sand. I had forgotten how, for every foot you step forward in a sand dune, you slip back two. Somewhere along the way, you catch up and overtake your loss, but the solutions to mathematical word problems always eluded me, and I thought I would never solve this one. Finally, at the top, winded and hot, I sat down facing the ocean.

I have always loved the Pacific and the coves of the northern California coastline. From the top of the dune, Monterey Bay slipped away from me in the swell and the foam of the waves, in the towering outbursts of rock crowned in seaweed. I took it all in as I tried to breathe a steadier rhythm and calm my racing heart.

"Mom," he said. "Let's somersault, Mom."

"Okay," I said. I was so unsuspecting. I watched his lithe body roll away from me down the dune, and I followed suit, only to find myself stretched flat on my back in the sand halfway down the dune, disoriented and stunned. You could have told me aliens had abducted me, and I would have believed you at that moment. The world had changed shape and reoriented itself in space. Time was a non sequitur, and I was alone in a whirling abyss of blue sky and ocean, unsure of which was which, convinced that every spring in my body was sprung.

And all because of a somersault.

I recovered and spent the rest of the day below the dune on the beach, trying to relax, but it had been a very telling experience. Somewhere in my mind, a little phrase kept playing like a bad recording— *You're not as young as you think you are.*

I'd heard it before. My mother and her friends had pointed it out to me for years, but, in my mind, I am always twenty-something, or some young, indeterminable age where limitations of anything don't exist, and even with my growing awareness, I am still faintly surprised when they surface.

When I lay stretched out in the sand, recovering from the somersault, I felt I had reached a turning point in my life. I realized that my body would not, of its own accord, maintain its elasticity. I might have to work at it if I wanted to continue somersaulting down sand dunes—or anywhere else. In that split moment, with the sky and the sea heaving interchangeably around me, I realized that the changes would only become more pronounced with time, that I was very, very mortal.

It was a split-second realization, almost more of a feeling than a thought, but it stayed like a brand in my brain, and it's there to this day.

Several months ago, I was in HEB with my oldest son, taking my blood pressure, a sign of aging and heredity I've accepted well enough to monitor. As I stepped away from the machine, I noticed the rack of reading glasses and stood before it for a minute or so, trying to read the directions. I've always had excellent eyesight and thought it a blessing because I would never have been able to hold onto a pair of glasses long enough to finish a book.

Still, I thought, of late, my vision's been a little blurry in the mornings, a little blurry in the evenings. I remembered my mother telling me that when I hit forty ... What could it hurt to try on a pair? I chose the lowest strength, placed them on my nose, and gasped as the letters jumped out at me, surreal in their clarity.

"Do they work?" asked my son. "Can you see better?"

"Yes," I breathed. "Yes, I can."

"Are you going to get them?" he asked.

"No," I replied. Firmly.

"Why not?"

"I don't need them yet."

He looked as if he wanted to ask another question but decided against it, something in his eleven-year-old soul understanding the value of discretion.

I have since bought a pair of those glasses but never wear them because they are not with me when I want to read.

Mentally, I've resisted the process of aging. Physically, my body plows through each day, oblivious to the fancies of my imagination, and ages as it will. I try to take good care of it. I have gone through stints of exercise, but I no longer jog, because my knees have asked me not to, and I have been cautioned to be kind to my knees.

I try to eat right, but these days, that's difficult. As a cook, I must taste the foods I prepare, and I've taught myself to taste only, resisting the temptation to finish off the bowl of lime mousse with raspberry sauce, the last half-pound of smoked tenderloin, the remaining slice of Gruyère cheesebread.

Reason insists on a balanced diet, a healthy exercise routine, plenty of sleep. Reason doesn't live in my house. It's a word I have to look up in the dictionary on occasion to refresh what remains of my memory.

My latest encounter with my body involves weight loss—or gain, as the case may be. I suddenly realized after a recent vacation that days of driving and three meals a day translated into an increased involvement with the numbers on my scale.

Already, before the vacation, I had noticed the ascending pounds. I don't know where they came from. My lifestyle hadn't changed appreciably in the last few years, and it used to be I could skip a meal or two, tell myself I was losing weight, and it would be gone. That doesn't work anymore, I have discovered.

So my sweetheart and I have embarked on a diet as the latest barricade against the ravages of age. It's a high-protein, low-carbohydrate diet, the one that half of America adheres to on any given day, and while it has many naysayers, it has many gainsayers, as well, and nobody says it doesn't work. A few say we may die in the process, but we are trying to live, and live with the diet, at that.

A person with some smattering of personal discipline, I have coaxed myself through the last two weeks by telling myself that few things are permanent, particularly diets. One of the few things that is permanent if you don't do something about it is your weight, I tell myself. I appeal to my vanity, which has taken on a new outlook as I try to age gracefully. I appeal to my desire to have grandchildren, to write the Great American Poem, to become a five-star chef. I appeal to the future.

And I cheat a little. I have an occasional glass of wine and wish I hadn't. I taste the borracho beans and dip my finger in the rum cake batter. I tell myself—moderation in all things, including diets. I never say never because my soul rebels at never and breaks every rule in the book, leaving behind a graveyard of good intentions.

So Jimmy and I are dieting. We are fixing garlic bread for other people and not eating it. We are drizzling apricot cake with rum-apricot glaze and passing it out with a smile. We are not ordering pasta, and order two salads as sides instead of a baked potato.

We are almost virtuous, except in our moments of weakness, when we dream out loud together about fresh fruits and home-made breads, spicy Mexican foods and sweet, soft spoonfuls of flan.

Instead we indulge ourselves in steaks and cheese and salads, chicharrones and smoked oysters. It goes against all I have ever learned, but the pounds are dropping. Within weeks, I tell myself, you won't be able to see me when I turn sideways.

My oldest says he will never go on our diet, because he couldn't have milk and cereal, tortellini, or pizza, the staples of his diet. I look at his slender body that still somersaults at will down any given hill, at his clear brown eyes that everyone says look so much like mine, and I resist the urge to say, *Just wait, my son.* Just wait. You are only as old as your body thinks it is.

Grapes

Summer's fruit is drying on its vines, the dusty mustang grape withered to a raisin, the vines giving up their weight to relentless sunshine. August is here.

Grapevines trace our seasons well. Native to these hills and valleys, they trail along fence lines, lace their way through oak and cypress, drape a condescending grace over cedar-post arbors that we build to tame them.

Despite the heat, we are working our way into fall, when the leaves redden with a blushing fury if we have an early cold snap, and the raisiny remains of the summer's grapes contrast their purple-black against that scarlet rage. If we chill slowly into winter, the leaves, merely yellow, droop and sift to the drying grass below.

In winter, in the silver air, the vines claim a starkness, a gray, wiry spin of tendril and muscle that twines around tree limbs, then drops and hangs, leaving off in midair—a sentence unfinished, an incomplete breath.

By spring, they've begun the greening, the early leaves unfurling from the gray bark, the clusters of grapes emerging from new growth. At first, the grapes are tiny, tight-fisted balls. On stiff stems, they break away from the vine in green miniature. They are promises to be kept, secrets that we know the answers to. As spring warms and the leaves broaden, the grapes swell in their green skins, crowd one another on the stem, hide in the tangling leaves.

By summer, the leaves have darkened. They soften the fence lines, shade the arbors with a deep-breathing green. Hang a swing on those cedar limbs and hide in the shadows. You're almost underwater in the cool loss of light.

And in July, the treasures appear—lush clusters of grapes begin to slip through the leaves in purple abandon. They tumble. They fall. They burst underfoot. Hedonistic, sensuous, they insinuate wine, a jewel-like jelly, a thick, sweet syrup. They intimate unfailing sunlight, lethargic heat. They beg to be picked, intact with their leaves, to be laid alongside a stout wedge of cheese and chewy, dense bread.

And it's here that the romance fails. This is Central Texas. Those romantic purple clusters are mustang grapes. Ever tried to eat a mustang grape? Ever tried to make wine with it? Pick it?

When it comes to eating, the mustang grape must be God's cruel joke on the grape world. The skins on those grapes are seriously thick, and the insides separate easily from the skins to leave a white pulp with large seeds and a noncommittal flavor.

I've never made wine with it, but I've tasted wine made from the grape, and, as drinkable wines go, I don't recommend it.

And I have picked it. Yes, I have picked it.

The mustang grape packs a reverence around our house. As a child, I remember the cotton bag, made from diapers stitched together, stained a deep royal purple, swinging from the lower branches of the oak outside the door. It held a mashed-up mess of mustang grapes that someone in our family had picked, and it dripped the purple juice into a metal pot in which it would later be cooked into jelly.

Picking the grapes was a kind of ritual. I hated it, but still, unwilling to buck the family tradition, even if just for the sake of maintaining it, I did pick the grapes.

I remember the outings well. My mother would start checking the grapes in June, commenting on the abundance of the crop, or the lack thereof—depending on the amount of rainfall we had in the spring.

Grapevines grew enthusiastically on our property, some of them draped over makeshift arbors, others climbing into the ethereal reaches of old oak trees. My mother knew where to find them and which ones would yield the most fruit, and when she determined that the grapes had hit their stride, she would rise early in the morning, muster her grape pickers, and head for the vines.

Remember, this was midsummer. She dressed us in long-sleeved shirts, in blue jeans, in gloves and boots and broad-brimmed hats. She parked the car or pickup under the vines, unloaded the ladder if she had one, and we all set to picking grapes.

There's something about the mustang grape that makes my hands and arms itch. I found that out young, the hard way. I didn't like the gloves and the long sleeves, so I took the gloves off and rolled up the sleeves. As I recall, I itched for days. More likely, it was only hours, but the memory has persisted for years.

It reinforced that hardest of lessons to learn—that my mother did what she did for a reason and not out of some cosmic sense of randomness. I'm not saying that grape picking drove the lesson home—I'm still learning it while trying to teach it to my children at the same time—but it scored points for my mother.

In the summer, grapevines exhibit an unfettered wantonness. With no fear of heights, they climb trees not meant for climbing. They reach for clouds and sunlight, for heaven, I believe. In January no one could imagine those stark, wintry vines exploding into so much greenery, taking over trees and fences and arbors with such an excess of ambition.

But they do, and, in so doing, they gift the less-revered creatures of this countryside with homes and hiding places. Danger lurks there. Snakes and wasps dwell in that mass of leaves. I was never bitten or stung while I picked grapes, but I was respectful. I had been stung by wasps, and I had seen the naked muscle of a snake looped around the limb of a cottonwood tree, barely visible in the light scattered through the leaves. I had a good enough imagination to see that same snake woven through the grapevines.

I picked gingerly and with trepidation, but I picked. It was strange work. Usually when picking fruit, you can indulge yourself in enough of it to justify the labor, but the mustang grape doesn't lend itself to that. No popping of the sweet, warm fruit into your mouth between handfuls. The rewards of mustang grapes came later.

It was hot, sweaty work in mid-July. My mother brought water and friends and relatives. Sometimes she hired people to help her. When I was older and eager to earn money, she even hired me. But always, she tried to be there herself. In years when she lived overseas and couldn't make it back in grape-picking season, my aunt saw to it that grapes were picked, cooked, and juiced, so that my mother could at least make the jelly for which she had become famous.

Because that was the point of all that heat and early-morning energy: grape jelly. It was a family tradition before I came along. My mother had watched her mother make it, probably even watched her grandmother make it. Back then, there was no electricity in these parts, and the grapes were boiled over the heat of a wood-burning stove in a kitchen with no fans or air-conditioning. At least by the time I came along, we dizzied the world outside with the wafting smell of grape juice spun from the kitchen by fans.

Grape jelly. It's a summer ritual, and successful rituals override discomfort. Perhaps they even thrive on it.

Grapes picked, my mother boiled them—skin, stems, and all—in big cauldrons, then poured the boiled mass into cotton bags made from diapers.

Once the juice was drained, it was boiled again with sugar, and lots of it. I once heard someone say that rhubarb pie was an excuse to pour sugar into a pie shell, and I believe the mustang grape must be a close cousin to the rhubarb stalk.

My mother is, in some ways, a purist. She doesn't believe in store-bought pectin, but coaxes the natural pectins from the fruit through cooking. Most of the time, she is successful and lines the kitchen table with dark, rich jars of trembling jelly. But sometimes, the pectin is recalcitrant and she lines the table with dark, rich jars of thick grape syrup, wonderful mistakes to pour across pancakes soaked in melted butter.

Then, of course, the jars must be sterilized and sealed, a hot process in itself. And sometimes, the jars don't seal, so the jelly must be refrigerated immediately and eaten soon. Those are the jars given to the first friends who walk through the door on jelly-making day, the friends who did us a favor or had the good luck to come to dinner.

When I was younger, the sealed jars were stored in cabinets and closets, then carted off to California, where we lived most of the year, where no one has ever heard of a mustang grape, where people think grapes are for eating and wine-making.

My mother gave the jelly for Christmas presents. She still does. When my parents moved to Japan, she hauled the purple jars across the Pacific and gave them to the Japanese, who loved them, who were charmed by the idea of the whole process — the whole picture of wide-open Texas fields, of achingly blue skies, of leafy sprawling vines, pointy-toed boots, and broad-brimmed hats.

And, finally, who could resist the jelly, with its tart sweetness spread across toast, pancakes, or the bowl of a spoon? Who could resist the taste of tradition?

Last month, I came across my mother and father in a field of drying grass and spent wildflowers. They were dressed in grape-picking garb and had driven an old pickup truck beneath the shade of an immense grapevine. They had started a little later in the day than planned, but the river lay just a few feet beyond the grapevine, and they would jump in when the grapes were picked. They couldn't let the season pass them by.

My mother tried to explain it, waved her arm past the soaring, trailing luxury of vine and grape and said, "It sort of gets you close to the earth, and you feel like you did the whole thing. You grew it, picked it, made it, and gave it to friends.

"It's very satisfying."

Amen.

Whippoorwill

Whippoorwill's Lament

"Do you know where your children are?"
The whippoorwill is crying.
Where has the nestling flown away?
What cats observed her flying?
And that is why the whippoorwill
She sings the saddest sound—
The long good-bye, the loud lament
Nest-builder on the ground.

— JIMMY ASH

We were walking the caliche path to the river, my friend and I, when a bird exploded from the cedars and flew straight at us. Startled, we jumped back, expecting it to veer, but it didn't. It careened its tattered flight between us like something demented, and we stepped to opposite sides of the path to let it by.

"A kamikaze bird," I whispered to my friend, thinking that really it might be a mother bird trying to distract us from her nest of babies. Or maybe it was sick, judging from its rough feathers. Maybe even rabid, if they make rabid birds.

The bird landed its unsettling flight in the middle of the path right behind us and sat huddled into itself and shaking. I stepped closer to get a better look and realized it was a baby bird,

171

new at feathers, new at flight. I thought it might be a dove, although its tail seemed a little short, but it was growing into some things and out of others, so proportions seemed irrelevant.

We watched it for a few minutes until I realized we were making it nervous. No one wants his first clumsy attempts at flight monitored by a foreign species, a species of questionable intent. No one wants to skid to the ground, winded and dazed, only to be hovered over by towering giants. So we left it there, hoping it would regain its composure and choose a less ragged path through the air next time.

As we neared the river, my nine-year-old son sped past us on his bicycle, towel streaming behind him, blond hair swept back, body as smooth as new growth will allow.

"Did you see the bird?" we asked.

"Yeah," he replied and headed for the water.

Then we heard the shouting. Angry it sounded, and loud. We stopped, stared at each other, and turned back toward the bird, which we couldn't see around the bend. That's when Jimmy loomed into view. My sweetheart is a big man with a booming voice and a soft heart.

"Did you see the bird?" we asked.

"A whippoorwill," he said. "A baby whippoorwill, and the cats were after it. I called them off before they got it."

I hadn't thought of the cats, the sleek golden pets who slide against our legs with love and move between the grasses with all the grace of snakes. I hadn't thought of how they perch along the railing on the deck and watch the birds flutter through the cypresses, listen to the canyon wrens float their descending scales along the creek.

Princes of patience. Masters of the waiting game. Bird watchers. I hadn't thought of them.

But they must have sensed from a distance the novelty of a flight that was plummeting to the hard caliche path, and they had come dressed for dinner, which, thanks to Jimmy, they didn't get.

The bird, he said, had mustered its courage, or its terror, just before the cat pounced, and taken off from the runway in an uneven flight to the cedars just beyond. Thwarted, the cats had sulked their way back up to the house.

I thought of that young bird all evening and into the next day. And I thought of its mother. Raccoons roam our neighborhood. Possums slip through the night. The neighborhood dogs trot back and forth along the trail to the river. Fire ants spread like disease. The cats own the land.

And the whippoorwill, the poorwill, the chuck-will's-widow — all the night singers, burdened with the patterns of their culture and their species, lay their delicate white eggs on the bare ground. As it turns out, this fledgling was probably a chuck-will's-widow. The whippoorwill nests farther north and farther east of Wimberley, singing its song through our hills only in late April on its way to somewhere else.

But the chuck-will's-widow mothers her nestlings on our ground. A friend has seen the nests and describes them as minimalist in their approach. No soft feathering, no shiny foil for decoration, no intricate basket weave. Just rocks and caliche with a scattering of forest debris. How the birds, the big nightjars, as they're called in the vernacular, protect their children from the predatory forces, I don't know.

Perhaps it is their camouflage. A humble brown, they blend into the forest floor like a rounded rock and cleave, immobile, to their nests, scaring up only at the last possible second.

I have woken many a summer evening and heard their echoing call across the river. The call and response. The gospel singers and survivors of the night.

Maybe that call is a prayer. Maybe it's like the one I say in my head when I see my oldest son studying his first patterns of flight. I, like the chuck will's widow, am grounded in my mothering and have tried, with limited wingspan, to shelter my sons. Sometimes, I think it's why I live here, why I have tried to escape the crowded streets of a more peopled world, why I have settled down amidst rock and caliche alongside the banks of the water.

That young bird scared up too soon, the experts say. But then, he was young, and timing is a learned process. The young are more spontaneous and less wary and remember only what their mothers taught them about holding still when they find themselves in the midst of the freeway they were warned against playing in.

The other day, my son brought home a CD he had proudly bought with his own money. I grew up on folk music and my father's old albums of the Sons of the Pioneers. Metal grates on my ears, and I studiously avoid listening to what has been called acid rock, heavy metal, industrial rock, urban rock. I'm not interested. I don't want to argue about it. I just don't want to listen to it. I had always thought I could live and let live, and anyone who wanted to listen to it could do so freely as long as they didn't make me participate.

This was different. I wasn't with my son when he bought the CD, but someone advised me to look at the lyrics, so when he was in school the next day, I did, and something in me changed forever. I couldn't breathe for the anger, for the incomprehension, and the fear. Anger at a world that could popularize the sentiments behind the lyrics. Anger at a store that would sell them to a child, or to anyone for that matter. Anger at a tide turning with such force that all the sheltering in the world will not withstand it. Incomprehension. Fear.

I cried all day. Even listened to the CD, to the sounds blaring so loudly from the speakers they drowned out the words I could not bear to read. I tried to tell myself that all generations differed over music, and that I was sounding like my parents and everyone else's parents twenty-five years ago. I tried to tell myself to calm down, that it was no big deal. I tried to tell myself a lot of things.

But in the end, I met my son at school, bought him an ice cream cone, sat down with him at a picnic table under the wide, blue, defenseless sky that shelters this changing world, and explained to him why we were taking the first CD he ever purchased back to the store. His eyes filled with tears, and I tried to explain why, as a parent, I had to do it, that I wasn't angry, that I loved him. I told him it was breaking my heart, too, and, finally, did he really like the music? Did he understand it?

No, he said. He hadn't listened to the words because he couldn't differentiate them from the noise of the album. But he liked the sound okay. Really, he said, he had wanted another album, but he didn't know who the artist was or how to find it, so he settled for this one because he had seen the cover before.

I breathed deep. "Okay," I said. "Let's take it back and find the other one." So we did. I quit crying, wiped my eyes, and found my vision altered. I felt like I had my nestling back — for a moment. Someone had warned me before the cat jumped, and that early, erratic attempt at flight had landed him back on the limb momentarily beside me.

I'm paying more attention now, but I cannot and should not stop the practice flights, hard as they are to watch. We bought summer clothes the other day, and he outfitted himself smartly in black from head to toe. Something in me wanted to cry — you're too young to dress yourself in black — but he did look good. The next day, he asked me to buy him a pair of sunglasses to complete the look.

I watched him through the day. The sunglasses came on and off, lost themselves at least once, and loaned a kind of aloofness, coolness to the whole picture. He wore the same outfit for two days running, washing it in between. "Please," I said, "be sure to vary your life. Don't give in all the way to black." He looked at me scornfully and wore a different set of clothes the next day.

But I could see it in the works, the gearing up for flight, the wings unfolding. I feel very strongly my ties to the ground, the vulnerability with which we all raise our children, and I wonder how it is that most of us make it through the early failures of our attempted flights.

I know I have to stand back some in the cedars with the chuck-will's-widow and watch. Still I reach out to cover him, and still he pulls in close to the shelter, but I can feel the restless air between us, and I am watching for the golden cats, for the raccoons and the possums.

The other night, as I drifted toward sleep, I heard through my open window the creek overflowing the dam and in the counterpoint of tree frogs and crickets, a voice — half song, half echoing chant — *Chuck-will's-widow . . . Chuck-will's-widow.*

I have decided that if the chant is the prayer, then the song is the hymn. The song is the thanks. The song is the warning. Nest builder on the ground.

 Ice

I've had enough. Waking these past mornings to a gray-and-silver world shouldering its way out of the dark, I lie beneath the fluff of covers and feel the chill rubbing against the windows like the cats who resist their outdoor status in winter and cry in their piteous voices that they are mistreated royalty, princes in a world of paupers who deserve the warmth of the indoors.

But, unlike the cats, the chill pervades, enters the house at will. It crawls along the floor and slips beneath the covers of the bed.

I lie there for a moment, caught between the edges of warmth and the edges of winter. If I don't move, I am insulated and useless, a floating zone of comfort that cannot last. If I stretch my leg, it is winter all over the bed, and I might as well get up and run for the shower, where I ruminate on how I wanted this weather in the heat of last August. How I couldn't wait. How winter teased the horizon like the promised land.

And now it's here. Now the world is stilled with cold, and I had forgotten how the feel of ice knifes through the body like the blood of an uncertain dream. I had forgotten the magnetism of the down comforter, the safety of a bed as the morning fogs at the windows and the trees emerge, each branch limned in silver, overhanging the frozen planks of deck below.

But growing up, they say, means attaining personal discipline. I lie in bed and think about that for a while before remembering I am supposed to be grown up, because if I am not, then who in this wintry fortress will be?

So I race for the shower, then paw through the tumble of sweaters I have not worn this year. Finally I head for the children's room to see how they have weathered the weather.

They are unaware of personal discipline and adhere only to comfort. They burrow beneath the blankets until they cannot be seen, their beds lumpy with pillows and unidentified hills and valleys. When I pull the covers back to locate their bodies, they are folded tight as fists around a fierce sleep, wrapped in thermal underwear and a hint of hibernation.

"Wake up!" I cry. "Look! The ground is white with—ice, or something like snow."

That always gets them. The hills and valleys flatten into bodies that rise beneath the blankets, make a beeline for the windows, where the cold breathes its frigid magic. There they begin their dance and their winter chant.

"I'm cold!" they cry, rocketing from bare foot to bare foot. "I'm cold! I'm cold! I'm cold!"

"That's why God made clothes," I explain, coaxing on socks and sweatshirts and pants as the crescendo rises, until nothing, it seems, will warm the chill that has crept through the window glass, the silver that has spread across the land like a life of loose change.

"Guys," I say, "guys, slow down. Put your clothes on, your jackets. Put on your shoes and go outside for a look. Winter can be beautiful. In North Dakota, this would be a banner day, a good-weather day. They would welcome this day in North Dakota."

They stare at me in disbelief, and the North Dakotans may as well join the ranks of unfed Chinese for all the good this weather will do them.

Winter breeds a strange hunger. My children don't eat most of the year. Bromeliads at birth, they concede only to occasional carbohydrates and then, I think, only to throw me off track. But winter has its own menu. "Hot chocolate," they beg. "French toast and waffles, pancakes and grapefruit. Cheese tacos, cheese omelets."

All of the above? I am incredulous. "All," they insist. They are hungry. For once in their lives, they are hungry. And cold.

"I have the heat on," I say. "It's not that cold in here."

The chant picks up. "I'm cold, I'm cold, I'm cold." They perch on tiptoe, balancing haunches on heels on stools in the kitchen, arms tethered to their chests in a lifesaving embrace, harnessing the body's heat—the classic winter pose, the upright fetal position. They rock back and forth as much as the small space on the stool will allow. "I'm cold, I'm cold, I'm cold," they chant. Sometimes, in the midst of the chant, they fall off the stools.

"Guys," I say, "you are so lucky you live in Texas."

Because there is ice on the ground, they do not have to attend school and are free to launch into the next phase of the chant, which is "What are we doing today?" Variations on that theme include "There's nothing to do."

I explain that I still have to work even though ice paves the driveway, and mentally rack my brain. What did I do as a child, I ask myself. Was I always bored? Didn't I find books to read? (Good books, surely. The entire *Encyclopedia Britannica*, Joyce's *Ulysses, War and Peace.* Mind-expanding books.) Weren't there always dolls to dress? Pictures to draw? Things to do? Self-righteousness climbs to a new high, outstripping the record-breaking cold. "When I was a child," I hear myself saying, "we didn't have Nintendos or Gameboys. When I was a child, we didn't have a TV set. I lived in New Jersey, where ice storms happened twice a day when I was a child, and I didn't have to walk to school in the snow, because there was too much of it. I even cut my ear on the ice one time and didn't cry.

"When I was a child and lived in the snow, I wore five layers of clothing to school and still remember the smell of wet wool in the cloak room. When I was a child ..."

My children stare at me blankly: a redhead and a blond—one a comic, the other deadly serious. Temperaments aside, neither is amused. I resign my memories to live with the North Dakotans and the Chinese.

We spend most of the next several days inside. The roads are icy, I'm told. Don't be a hero. Don't brave them. So I write in my bedroom instead of at the office, wrapped in blankets and warmed by small heaters. When I give myself the space to think about it, I see the electric meter whirring outside, delighted by the cold, a dizzy dance of electricity.

My children watch television, play electronic games I don't understand, and build elaborate transportation systems that stretch across the breadth of the living room, ensuring safe passage for the wooden trains and uncertain destinations for the inhabitants of the house. They eat lots of cereal and pizza, even though I offer them such classic winter fare as split pea soup and pot roast.

The cats cry at the windows. I stare at their yowling mouths open to the frosting air and wonder if cats freeze in the cold or if they muster their legendary resources and find a nest in the old clothing stuck in the loft in the garage. I feel sorry for them, let them in briefly, and the one named Tigger scratches my youngest son. I let them back out.

As evening approaches, the redhead decides he wants a friend over.

"It's nighttime," I say.

"So?" he says.

We play Scrabble and poker and lose track of time. I read to them, stroke restless heads, explain that there will be no school again tomorrow but they still have to go to bed. "Wintertime does not preclude sleep," I say. They stare at me with the vacancy of small, bored, caged animals who have not had enough exercise. I wonder if children sleep in North Dakota.

I drink a glass of red wine and watch the cold etch promises on the window. *This is Texas,* I think it says. *This will all be over soon.*

The next day we start again, but, by late afternoon, I decide to brave the roadways to go to the store. While appetites have abated somewhat, we still need milk and eggs, and how bad could the roads be? When I arrive at the store, I wonder what has happened in my absence. Shelves are stripped of merchandise, and the employees wear a slightly stunned expression.

"Have a little run on food?" I ask. Apparently so.

It's a strange psychology this freeze brings, a built-in fear based on something other than the weather. Primal, maybe. A need to be prepared for the worst. With a bad freeze, it could be a day or two before people get back to the store.

True enough. I place some of the last eggs and milk into my basket, settle for a loaf of white bread, and speculate on being lost in my pantry for days. How long, I wonder, could I last on artichoke hearts and anchovies, on black currant jelly and chipotle sauce, on Campbell's Soup and shiitake mushrooms?

Maybe, I speculate, as I load a few unnecessary items prompted by the weather into my cart—items like split peas for split pea soup and bananas for Bananas Foster—maybe people are a little excited by the thought of cold weather. They dream of what people in places like North Dakota eat when it's cold, and their dreams strip the grocery shelves.

This is Texas, where the main theme song is heat, so cold weather is an anomaly that must be celebrated with marshmallows and hearty soups, with rich desserts and hot, spiked drinks.

Back home, friends stop by to tell me of cars spun out on the roads, of frozen pipes and stuffy noses. My children create a homemade sled by freezing two serving trays together and sliding around on the deck overlooking the creek. I remind them that it's cold outside and they should wear jackets. They look at me like I've lost it.

It's not cold, they say. Why do I think it's cold outside? Their hands and lips are verging on blue, and they are not cold. Night hovers in the silvery air, and the chill rubs against the windows. I decide they would do well in North Dakota.

After dinner, I haul out the cards and the Scrabble board again, and the children start to fight. I put my head in my hands and say small, heartfelt prayers to the God who created Texas, this land of heat and summer. "Remember," I say, "what sunshine feels like? Remember that blue blaze of sky?"

"Cabin fever," says my friend, patting my hand. "It's a relative thing. It's filled with relatives."

Our children race through the house, dismantling the chaos that started two days ago. I nod. He's right. I pronounce bedtime and force sleep on the world.

The next morning I wake to water dripping from the eaves, where there were icicles the night before. We will have school today, and I will venture back to work. The sky will blaze a clearing blue. The children will take their coats to school and forget them because it won't be cold in the afternoon. The cats will bask in the sun and forget about the indoors. The store will restock its shelves.

And it's a good thing. Because this is Texas, and I just heard that whistling in on the heels of all this balmy weather we've been having for the past day or so, this weather that would occasion swimsuits in North Dakota, is a blue norther. The cold kind where you drip your faucets, light your fires, stock up on marshmallows, and play Scrabble and poker.

Maybe I'll be better at it this time. I've had a rehearsal. I've stocked my shelves. I know all the verses to the song, and I'm feeling a little jaded.

But at least I know it'll be over soon. After all, this is Texas.

# Spring

A couple of days ago, as I was driving my small redheaded son to preschool, he erupted in the back seat, escalating immediately to the top of the scale.

"My buds!" he screamed. "I forgot my buds!"

"Bugs? What bugs?" I said, confused.

"No, my buds! On the trees! The pink ones! I wanted to show my class! We're talking about signs of spring!"

And then I remembered the graceful spread of the redbud tree in our yard, how the child had stood beneath its pink shade and fingered the lowest branches in fascination, wondering at the tiny blossoms clustered along its dark skin.

So I pulled over, turned the car around, and headed back toward the house to pick a small gesture of pink for him to take to his class. He carried it in front of him when we arrived, and everyone smiled. The tears had dried. He was all red curls and pink blossoms as he proudly told everyone that these were the flowers of a pinkbud tree.

His teacher was enchanted. How could anyone resist a child in love with spring?

I am in love with spring. I think almost everyone is. True, this year our winter was so negligible that the segue into the season of rebirth was low-key and undramatic, but at least March had graced us with one cold spell to formalize the closure of winter.

So now, in the last part of the month, with the official advent of spring upon us, we have emerged into truly springlike weather. Days have warmed, almost past the point of springlike, into the 80s. Trees are softening their stark limbs into blossoms, and the cypress along the creek and river are shaded in iridescence—from one angle, gray with winter; from the other, mossy with the first nudgings of green.

People look for different signs of spring. I have a friend, Dea Albertson, who swears that if in a short span of time you see two or more dead skunks along the roadside, you can count on another cold spell or two before spring sets in, and she says it held true again this year.

Or when the mountain laurel in front of the Ozona Bank blooms, you know you can plant safely.

Pat Benner adds a little Texas lore: "The old-timers where I come from [Wharton] look for blooms on the native pecan as the absolute proof of spring, and the people south of here say you can't fool a mesquite tree."

Fishermen might count spring as the run of white bass through the cold currents of Rebecca Creek or the Pedernales River.

Sun worshipers unfold their lawn chairs in the shallows of the Blanco, unroll their towels, baste their bodies in oil, and sleep the dreams of sun-drunk waters and warm brown skin.

Spring is a brief respite in Texas, too brief by many standards, with summer hanging on every rising degree, but it is a respite, and we respond. We can't help it. I believe the seasons course through our bodies with the same force they plow through the great outdoors.

I can feel it. I can feel the loosening of the limbs as the weather warms, the edging toward the doors and open windows, trying to get a feel of the air against my skin. Staying inside is an effort. I dream in colors and foods—peach blossom and strawberry, asparagus, butter yellows, and endless, tumbling blues. Fields of bluebonnets, acres of sky. Whipped-cream drifts of cloud and cotton, the fine white fog of flowering pear.

In springtime, something in me needs the earth. Like the pull of a magnet, it draws my hands to it, to the damp leaf smell of the crumbling soil.

I cannot pass a nursery without the urge to buy seedlings. I'm not the only one. Tim Thompson at King Feed says watching gardeners buy seeds and starts is a little like watching a starving man in the grocery store.

"Our business has just been wacko for a couple of weeks," he says. "It's been a struggle the past few weeks to keep things in that people want to plant."

Plants show promise, says Tim. They promise riots of color, groundcover to soften this hard land, sweet fruits.

"Gardeners are mostly forward-thinking people who see the promise in things," says Tim. "You have to be to be a gardener. If you're only interested in the finished product, you can go to the florist. But it takes a lot of dedication to posterity and to the future to plant a seedling oak tree. I think it's a statement of faith in the future to plant trees."

The sun scatters down through the loose weave in Tim's straw hat.

"I just love all the thousands of millions of stories of resurrection in all the trees and plants budding, pollinating, blossoming."

He scratches at his white beard and grins. In springtime, he says, philosophy blooms right alongside the prairie verbena.

I used to garden when I had more time and remember coming on one of the signs of spring in the tall grass of the asparagus patch. I was walking the garden with my neighbor and my oldest son, who was about three at the time, when I came on a patch of fluff caught at the base of the grasses.

"Look," I said to my neighbor, "some animal must have gotten in a fight and left a piece of fur behind."

My neighbor laughed. "Pick up the fur," he said. "Look at what's underneath."

So we did and found three baby cottontails curled into each other, a tight maze of earth-brown softness that I could have held in the palm of my hand if I had scooped them out of their hollow.

But I left them alone, returning every few days to check on them. I saw their eyes open, watched them outgrow the hollow and, within a week, leave the nest for the tastier world of the garden.

My neighbor thought I was crazy. "You missed your chance," he said in amazement. "You could have wiped out three of your competitors right then and there, and you let them go."

He had a point. Bunnies had chewed holes in the frilly new lettuce, beheaded my early attempts at green beans, and lunched on the tiny fingers of asparagus that poked through the mulch. The elephant-proof fence that we had erected around the garden kept the elephants out, not the bunnies.

But it was spring, and my young son was enchanted with the babies. So was I, and we let them live. My son named them—Strawberry Helmet, Sick Saw Grass, and Asparagus. Sometimes, when a flash of cotton races the roadway for the bushes near the garden, I wonder if I'm not seeing one of them in action.

In another season, distraught with heat or clenched with cold, I might not have felt such mercy. In another season, I would not have seen them.

They say spring is a fever. I say it's a dreaming, a waking, a stretching, a deep breath that cleanses and lengthens the soul.

Trip West

L ast week, I partook of an American tradition. Holding my trepidation at bay, I loaded my children and all their paraphernalia into the back of my van and headed west on the highways of America.

It sounds simple enough. Generations of families have flooded the roads as summer hits its stride, but the longest trip I had ever taken with my boys was a jaunt down to the Gulf Coast at Rockport. Three hours can take on the dimensions of infinity when the recurring musical theme hits on the high whine of "Are we there yet?"

This time, we were headed for northern New Mexico, and I was worried. I explained to the boys it would be a long trip. I promised them car games, books, music, and junk food. Essentially, I bribed them.

And, in the great parental tradition, I threatened. We would have no fighting, I said. All it took to end the trip was a U-turn in the road, and I knew how to make a U-turn. My oldest son, Malone, who is eight, has an analytical bent. "What if a U-turn is illegal at that point?" he asked.

"It doesn't matter," I said. "I will risk it."

"You would risk breaking the law to turn back?" he asked with amazement.

"I would," I said, suddenly envisioning the world's shortest road trip.

The little one, Cameron, who is five, considered the threat, stuck his thumb in his mouth, and declined to comment.

I hit the stores before we left and came home loaded down with maze books, kids' travel books, decks of cards, boxes of cereal, and several tapes. I asked my friends to pray for our sanity and safety. The rest would follow, I assured them. I made last-minute phone calls, tried to pay last-minute bills so we would have electricity and water when we returned, made lists and lost them, and started out two hours later than I had originally planned. Our goal was to reach Fort Stockton the first night, meet my cousin there the next morning, and caravan into Los Alamos, where my other cousin lives.

The plan worked well enough, although I pulled to the side of the road outside of Johnson City as the bickering in the backseat began to surge toward the front seat.

"Why are you stopping, Mom?" Malone asked.

I muttered something about seeing if the road was clear for a U-turn, and the boys became immediate best friends, teammates, angels who would never fight again. "No, Mom, no," they begged in unison. "Please, Mom, no. We'll stop. We weren't fighting. We were just pretending, practicing, anything but fighting. Don't stop, Mom. Please."

It was convincing, so we headed west through the rocky hills and cedars of Johnson City, Stonewall, Fredericksburg, and Junction. We passed the signatures of the drought — the peach-less orchards, the empty roadside stands — and gradually the land opened on either side of us, stretching out into the interminable flatness of West Texas.

As we traveled, a strange peace began to take hold. I let go of the fear and began to feel a companionship with my boys. We were on an adventure together. Something about the highway and the shadows deepening through the flatlands began binding a spell. Cameron was entranced by the sleeping bags in the back of the van, the pillows, the idea of his own space, and he stretched out for a long nap. Malone climbed into the front seat, plugged "Rockin' Robin" into the tape deck, and rocked through the scrub and sand of the desert just east of Sonora.

He was fascinated by the play of clouds across the land, wanted to know why some splotches of desert were darker than others. I explained cloud shadows and broken promises of rain. He was skeptical. Was I sure, he asked, that the sands weren't just darker in some places than others?

I had forgotten the freedom of travel through open spaces. I had forgotten how the desert opens like a limitless heart to the nuance of rolling sky. As night approached, the sands, bound back from the road by barbed-wire fencing, deepened their desolation to a blue length of land and the skies burned to acres of gold. It was a canvas so blank it begged a story, a dream to give it definition, to give it context in a world increasingly painted in the uniformity of commerce and convenience.

We stopped in Sonora for dinner, and Cameron burned his arm on the sizzling plate of enchiladas the waitress placed before him. Strangers came to our rescue, a kind woman with a glass of ice to rub on the burn, the young waitress with infinite patience. She'd seen the look of the highway traveler before.

"We've come a long way," I explained as I held my sobbing son.

"I know," she said, and she smiled. "I can tell."

That left the final haul to Fort Stockton and the motel. As we drove back and forth on the interstate, trying to figure out which exit to take, Malone turned to me, his face full of dread. "You're lost," he said. "You don't know where you're going."

I had to laugh, and I pointed out the motel signs to him, explaining that I had missed the exit, that we'd catch it at the next pass, but I could see the fear in his eyes. A child of exactitude, he saw the night unraveling like a long black scarf across the desert. He saw the stars scattered in a random fling across the sky, and he didn't know where he was.

He wasn't the only one. As we doubled back toward the lights of Fort Stockton, Cameron asked if we were still in America.

"Yes," I said. "Not only are we still in America, we're still in Texas, although some people don't see them as one and the same."

"What do you mean, Mom?"

"Never mind."

The motel came next, and the boys were delighted. Something about motel rooms invites bed-jumping, the pulling to and fro of curtains, fiddling with locks, with TV channels.

They explored every inch of the room, and Cameron decided he would sleep on the shelf above the closet space until I pointed out the likelihood of falling out in the middle of the night.

In the morning, Malone plugged in to cartoons while we waited for my cousin to arrive, and Cameron headed out to the unheated swimming pool, a diversion that lasted long enough for him to figure out it was cold. I stood in the early-morning air of Fort Stockton, surrounded by the dry, scoured smell of desert, and felt the miles unroll before me, felt a timelessness settle in.

When my cousin arrived, we ate breakfast at McDonald's, then headed west on 285 toward Pecos, a town that claims a river, late-season cantaloupes, the haunt of Judge Roy Bean, the world's first rodeo, and proximity to the New Mexico border.

As we crossed into New Mexico and more desert, the loneliness hit me. Malone counted mirages, and my eyes sought out the breaks in the distance, the occasional outcropping of trees, punctuated with a windmill and maybe a house that looked as if it had not seen people in so long, the memory had atrophied to broken glass and splintered wood. Sometimes, mountains insinuated themselves, shadows on the horizon, never materializing, disappearing like the slick outlay of watery mirages along the pavement. Sometimes, we came across clusters of pump jacks bobbing their pointed heads toward the oil.

"Smells like Luling," said Malone.

"Smells like money," I countered.

Those were the stretches of no-man's land, where an occasional antelope grazed the meager weeds along the fence line, where cows hunched close to the hot earth like rounded boulders in the sand. It was a land harsh in its severity, its lack of compromise, a land of desert dreams that stared out of broken or boarded-up windows. Dreams have a way of disappearing, of lingering like smoke after fire, behind shredded curtains, reminders of the violence of sleep and neglect, but echoes, only echoes of the moment.

We passed a solitary restaurant, closed and dusty, no houses in sight, a loner by the side of the road. Who put it there, and why? What dreams died when the water went away or the oil pumped dry or the cars didn't stop?

Malone was glued to his travel book, memorizing the state

capitals and birds and flowers. Occasionally, he glanced up to search out the license plates of different states and marvel at the distances people travel in their cars. Frequently, he reset the tape for "Rockin' Robin."

We passed a grove of trees in the distance and a ramshackle house, the only sign of life a weathered pickup truck that might have been as abandoned as the house, "Malone," I said, "what kind of people do you think live out here?"

I was aiming for something abstract, the fresh philosophy of an eight-year-old mind, and I got it. He looked up, took note of his 102nd mirage, glanced at the trees and the surfeit of sand and the sun.

"Hot people," he said with conviction. "Hot and sweaty people."

Twenty miles east of Vaughn, my van broke down. As I tried to pass a car, I glanced down at my speedometer and noticed I was losing speed. When I finally made it around the car, I pulled over, my van jerking and grabbing to a stop. When I tried to start it again, it moved at about three miles an hour, with the accelerator flat on the floor. My cousin stopped ahead of me, and together we stared at the inscrutable engine. Cameron slept his desert dreams in the back seat, and Malone agitated alongside the vehicle, his dreams of perfection awry in the desert with a broken van.

I tried to calm him. We were fortunate, I said. We had cousins along. They could always take us into Vaughn. At least we were not stranded. And after all, wasn't this part of the American summer-vacation dream? The nightmare part?

We waited in the desert, leaned against the car, perused the owner's manual, laughed in helplessness, then started the car up again and found it drove just fine, took us all the way through the other side of Santa Fe before it broke down again.

The van actually made it into Los Alamos that evening, and in the week that followed, we replaced the gas filter, relieved that it was not more serious. That week was filled with small children, mostly boys who ran three miles for our every one as we took them through national monuments and down forest paths. They climbed 140 feet of ladders to see the kiva at the top of the Bandelier Monument, raced around a reservoir at twilight, chased tumbleweeds through gulches, played with cousins, fought with cousins, had moments of rare grace and minor meltdowns.

I found that, spending time with them without the constraints of clocks and school and work, I loved them more than I thought possible. I guess I already knew that, but responsibilities can coat the heart in distraction, unfocus the reason and priority that set the responsibilities in motion in the first place.

It was cool in New Mexico by our standards—dry and majestic. While forest fires had ravaged the countryside and much of the national park area was closed, still the spirit of those mesas climbing into mountains, the red rock of the land, the scent of piñon pines and Douglas firs overwhelmed the senses.

This was the "Land of Enchantment," as the yellow-and-red license plates claimed, a land where people have gravitated for centuries, sensing a timelessness in the air, in the soil that rises in reds and purples to form monuments to the soul. It is a magic so lyric it surrounds itself in desert, as if the approach and the departure must not interfere with the landscape of the heart.

We climbed winding roads through tiny towns, through the slight mist of rain, the first in months, that released a damp perfume from the ground. The colors of the cliffs mirrored sunrise, and the streams curved like secrets through forest grass.

And yet, winding those roads, I felt very much the tourist and questioned the truth of the masses seeking the spirit in commercialized Kokopellis and coyotes howling at the moon. The spirit so sought-after still hovers in the landscape and breathes the air of early-morning pines, but the details of the culture now march across t-shirts, through gift shops, along the expanse of billboards. I stared past the required adobe houses of Santa Fe, the carefully crafted beauty, and half admired the foresight of preservation. At the same time, I felt a sadness. Money has driven out the culture that created what the money preserves.

We did the tourist things—drove the wrong way up Canyon Street in Santa Fe, bought expensive chili powder in Chimayo, toured the science museum in Los Alamos to examine the mystery of salvation and devastation that was the Manhattan Project, drank margaritas in the desert, and breathed the damp, pine-laden air of thunderstorms.

And then we turned the van toward home. The trip back through the desert was less of an adventure—the van didn't break and the mirages became old news. Around Carlsbad, the winds picked up, buffeting the sides of the van and sending low-flying clouds of sand across the road. The sky yellowed, and the rain broke from the clouds shredding into veils of dark water in the distance.

My five-year-old cousin, who had agreed to ride with us into Carlsbad, took in the weather and decided he needed to make a pit stop so he could use the facilities and get back in the car with his father. I pointed out to him that we had just stopped, there were no facilities, and his father was two cars ahead of us. He then informed me he was getting car sick. I offered him the front seat, and he told me he had strep throat. I pointed out the rainstorms in the distance, and he told me they were tornadoes, not rainstorms. I said we were lucky to be watching them from a distance and turned on "Rockin' Robin." His symptoms disappeared.

We hit every McDonald's the highway yielded up, trying with great fervor to collect enough stickers to win their latest promotional—the Monopoly game. As I switched, in desperation, from burgers to salads at the last stop in Fredericksburg, I told my cousin that we had become victims of one of the great commercial manipulations of America. We were behaving just as McDonald's intended for us to behave. Malone did win a free cheeseburger, and he ate it, so all was not a loss.

Sometimes leaving offers new perspectives. I realized as we left the desert behind us in Junction that the magic we were approaching, the greenery and the kindness of trees, was the magic of home. We had survived our road trip into the Great American West, and we still loved one another. We had been gone a week and still recognized faces back home. The town was intact.

Later, I put my arms around Cameron and asked him what his favorite part of the trip was. His eyes never left the television screen, but he put his small arms around my neck and managed the best manipulation of all.

"You, Mom," he said.

Valentine's Day

It was a matter of pride in our family that we did not give out purchased valentines. None of those cardboard cards with perforated edges and cartoon characters professing love for us. We were creative, and we put our hearts into our cards.

For a while, at least, I thought everyone did the same. I even thought that the cardboard cards meant what they said, that my classmates were all in love with me and each other. I actually thought that was possible.

And then I remember the year when commercialism entered my life. As one of the few children whose valentines were made by hand, I was the object of bewilderment and some derision. Why would someone bother to go to the trouble of making a valentine when they could buy one? Were they too poor to afford a book of punch-out valentines? Did they have nothing better to do than sit at home and make valentines? Were they weird?

No, my mother told me. We weren't poor. We had plenty to do to keep us busy. And we weren't weird. We just believed in creativity and sincerity and making things from scratch.

We didn't much believe in forsaking quality for convenience. We didn't believe in store-bought valentines with canned messages, cheap thrills, or dried potato flakes. We believed in the real thing.

It was a valuable lesson. One that has both helped and hindered me through this seasonal journey.

As a child, I wanted to believe that the world and all that was in it was made from scratch. Shortcuts seemed like cheating. Professions of love were always true, and love was supposed to last forever.

Well, over the years, I've learned a few shortcuts. I've learned that convenience and quality don't have to be mutually exclusive. I've learned the world isn't black and white. I've learned that the inscriptions on homemade and store-bought Valentines aren't necessarily true. And I've learned that love doesn't always last forever.

By the time I reached high school, I wasn't taking heart-covered shoeboxes to school with me anymore. I was just taking my heart. I was hoping the one I loved that particular month would do something wildly romantic to prove his love. Sometimes he did, and sometimes he didn't.

Always one to swing on the gates of expectation like an acrobat, I was either deliriously happy or tunneling through the root cellars of despair. No sense in matching metaphors. When romance didn't blossom in the hard, cold ground of February, any measure of sense was a lost space probe. I was the victim of a failed heart.

I got over that, too. By the time I matriculated into higher learning, I had gained perspective on the world and had my index finger hooked around a dry sense of humor. Roses were good and all that. So was candy. Champagne was wonderful any time of the year. It still is.

I accepted valentines gallantly and with a touch of ennui, as befitted an aspiring poet and actress. The world must wreak havoc on the heart, and the heart must develop a faulty shield before it can be dealt with in an artistic sense. Too much giving in to the lushness of love results in a Hallmark greeting card, we wordmasters thought.

Our shields were truly faulty. Most are. We fell in love, and we fell out of love. We got our feelings hurt, and the ennui was a posture, at best. We still loved roses. We still loved love.

And now, well, now the postures have slid away like old skins. I don't have the time or energy to maintain them. I don't see the point. Some years, I buy my sons books of valentines from the store and feel a deep sense of relief when all we have to do is sign names and address envelopes. Convenience has its value.

Other years, I feel the need to hunt down the doilies and the gold foil, pull out the scissors and the glue. It feels good to create the world from scratch.

And Valentine's Day? These days, I have someone who loves me and makes me cards on February 14. Sometimes, he brings me a full red rose. Sometimes he just holds me.

But these days, I have learned to temper the expectation so that it becomes a broader perspective and welcomes gifts of love throughout the year.

I have learned to love the gift of a dozen sun-filled eggs from my friend's barnyard, the anonymous thank-you card from someone I wish I could thank, the fine food and the games of Scrabble with good friends, the donations of time when I am too busy to ask for it, the patience of friends and family, the words of compassion and even wisdom from my children, the companionship of my dog.

I have learned that people need candlelight and chocolate, lace and whispered promises in the gray light of February. I have learned that those bright tokens are always in demand. I have learned that valentines made from scratch can take the form of more than doilies and construction paper.

I have learned that we should give valentines and all that they imply all year long.

Easter

How do you cast the impression in the stone that becomes a tradition? How do you work the gears of memory so that the final perspective laces the snapshots together with laughter?

I have traditions from my own childhood that I have left behind, some with more regret than others, and other traditions have held in there with a vengeance.

Until recently, my mother sent me a chocolate bunny from 2,000 miles away every Easter, or she called relatives and asked them to put one at the foot of my bed. I think she gave up on that when I started having children.

At Christmas, until I stopped returning to my childhood home every year for the holidays, I caroled with a group of people I had known as long as I can remember, then settled into what was almost a midnight dinner—the adults, ravenous; the children, asleep on the pile of coats on someone's bed, too tired to eat.

We called it the Goose Dinner, and there was always one boney goose to commemorate the occasion—one boney goose and a couple of turkeys to make up the balance. But it was a holiday tradition, and if I were visiting before Christmas, I would go caroling and eat goose again.

It seems so many traditions are built around holidays, and I have been working hard at creating a new set of traditions since my children were born. Many of them are predictable, cultural traditions. Some of them ride with persistence off of bright memories. And some of them are downright stupid.

I think those are the ones I like the best. When I think of them, they make me giggle. In a world bound by the responsibility of logic and reason, where even clowns go to school to learn their trade, uncontrollable giggling is a magical release.

Several years back, my neighbor and I were planning Easter dinner, a shared tradition that usually involved pale pink slices of spring lamb rubbed with rosemary, tender shoots of bright green asparagus afloat in lemon butter, and new potatoes crusted in garlic and mint.

We set tables under the trees with wildflowers and roses, and the whole world seemed draped and shaded in wisteria, as if we had walked into the glasswork of a Tiffany lamp.

We were sharing a bottle of wine and trading details of the dinner, talking about Easter egg hunts and the best stands of wildflowers, when we both realized that Easter was closer than we had thought, and we had not yet purchased even the green plastic grass to line our children's Easter baskets.

In Wimberley, that can be a problem. Holidays are best planned ahead because the trappings of the season disappear quickly from local stores, and San Marcos suddenly seems farther and more impossible to reach than the mere twenty minutes it takes on a normal day.

Panicked, we left the house for the local grocery and found no Easter grass, no chocolate eggs, not even a jelly bean. So we punted.

We opted for the pastel look and went for Pixy Stix and SweetTARTS. I think we might have cached a chocolate bunny or two earlier in the month, so the baskets were not entirely devoid of Easter's more pagan icons, but it was an odd assortment of Easter candy that lined the baskets that year.

We were having fun, though. We were laughing our way through the store, looking for surprises that the children would enjoy — surprises that could somehow be linked to what was traditionally marshmallow chicks, foil-wrapped eggs, and small toys lost or broken before the day was out.

And then I found them, the perfect Easter basket gift — a small bottle of the palest pink pickled pigs' feet.

It would help to understand that pickled pigs' feet were kind of a joke in our family. When my children, who resist eating at every turn of the road, asked what we were having for dinner, I often told them we were having pickled pig's feet.

They followed that response with an inevitable howl— "Mommmm! Really. What are we having for dinner? And there is no such thing as pickled pigs' feet! Why would anyone pickle a pig's foot?"

"Oh," I always told them, "how wrong you are. There is such a thing, and people pickle them because they like them. Your own grandfather says he likes them. Ask him."

So they did, and he said that, in fact, he was very fond of pickled pigs' feet. He just hadn't had the opportunity to eat one in a while.

I looked at those clean, compact bottles of pickled pigs' feet. I took them off the shelf and admired their pale pink hue. I noted their reasonable price and thought of the way they would fill up an Easter basket, and I bought them.

As my neighbor and I drove home, we talked about how our children would wake with surprise to find the Easter bunny had stretched his reach beyond the obvious this year. We talked about how delighted they would be to see that even something that has been around as long as the Easter bunny has his moments of creativity.

When my children awoke on Easter morning, they were surprised. Their delight, I think, was dubious. They gave a nod to the predictable—the chocolate bunnies that I had the foresight to buy before Easter fled the stores. They cheerfully accepted the packages of SweetTARTS and the long stems of the Pixy Stix.

But they balked at the pigs' feet.

"What are these?" they shrieked in disgust, letting the jars slip from their fingers onto the bedcovers.

"Pig's feet," I said. "Pickled pigs' feet."

"Mommmmmmmmm! They are not! There is no such thing as pickled pigs' feet! And you know it!"

"Oh, but there is," I said. "Look closely."

So they did. As little boys, they possess a kind of delving curiosity that compels them to disassemble things and reach into the bowels of machinery to see how the world is organized, I presume.

They began to unscrew the tops of the bottles.

"No! Wait!" I said. I hadn't thought this far along, and somehow I knew that my boys, who eat only the most bland of foods, would not appreciate the sour tang and firm crunch of the pigs' feet. "Why don't we give them to Grandpa?"

It was an inspired suggestion. After that, they even believed that the soft pink-and-white things floating in the bottles were pigs' feet and seemed more inclined to study the briny anatomy of pigs than to hunt for Easter eggs.

When Grandpa came strolling through the wisteria, they couldn't wait to greet him—two fair and shining Easter boys, racing through the flowers with pickled pig's feet in their hands. Grandpa could not resist and opened a bottle then and there, attacking the unlikely-looking food with a fork and knife and offering to share with anyone who would take him up on his generosity.

But no one seemed inclined. Saving their appetites, they said. So he took his pickled pigs' feet home with him.

When the next year came around, I had learned my lesson about last-minute holiday shopping and filled respectable baskets with green Easter grass and chocolate eggs and jelly beans. But nestled into all that tradition was the start of a new tradition—two bottles of the palest pink pigs' feet you have ever seen.

The kids were livid.

"Mommmmmm!" they screamed.

"Hey, guys," I said. "Talk to the Easter bunny."

And so it has gone from year to year. Each Easter has had its share of differing details. We make changes in the plans. When it rains, we move the tables inside. Sometimes we have salmon instead of lamb. This year, the dogs ate the Easter eggs before the kids could find them, and we had to implore the Easter Bunny to return and hide plastic eggs.

But we have cemented our Easter tradition.

When my kids awoke this Easter, it was to a basket brimming with chocolate and jellies and bunnies and pink pickled pigs' feet.

"Mommmmmm!" they shrieked. "Why, Mommmm?"

"Because it's a tradition," I say. "And it's one you will always remember. You will say to your own children, 'When I was little, always, in my basket at Easter, there was a small jar of the palest pink ...'"

"Mommmmmm!" they roared.

Memories and traditions. It's a wonder how anything ever gets set in stone.

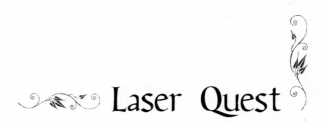 Laser Quest

I am not a warrior. I never really imagined myself to be one, but I tried on the concept the other day and found it didn't fit.

I've been working pretty hard lately, trying to find the portal to this blazing economy, and I've been missing my boys. I see them at breakfast and discuss the vagaries of the weather and their wardrobe—how hot it's going to get, whether they should wear shorts in February, why they have to wear socks to school, and why they can't wear the striped shirt with the madras shorts.

I see them when I pick them up from school. I listen to their discourses on Pokémon trading and their repetitive chorus of "There's nothing to do!"

I explain to them that even though I work at home, I'm still working. I pull them close and feel their frustration, just as they feel mine. I sense the need for some kind of bonding beyond the basics, beyond the task of mothering that tries to coax or cram civilization down the throats of my beautiful pagans.

I sense the need to participate in their world.

So Sunday afternoon, I lay on the couch and listened to possibilities of how we could spend our afternoon. In front of me, three boys and a man, ranging in age from nine to fifty-four, explored their fantasies of a Sunday-afternoon spent driving go-carts, playing laser tag or video games, or climbing Enchanted Rock.

I closed my eyes and heard the ocean in the distance. I

dreamed myself onto a beach with a long, sweet book. I smelled the salt marsh. In the foreground, my children played. They built sandcastles and picked up shells. They curled their bodies into the foaming waves, then washed up on the beach to stretch beside me in the sand.

They called the go-cart track but discovered that the track had already found the portal into the blazing economy and was charging exorbitant prices for the privilege of eating dust and listening to engines whine. *Good for them,* I thought.

"Mom! Mom!" they cried. "We've decided what we want to do. We want to drive to Austin and play laser tag!"

The beach receded. The sweet book faded. The boys—the nine-year-old, the twelve-year-old, the fifteen-year-old, and Jimmy—all stood before me, grinning. They'd made a decision. We would all drive to Austin and be warriors for twenty minutes.

I demurred. I would take a book and read in the car. I would browse Highland Mall. I would be there when they emerged from their twenty-minute war, then I would come home and fix them dinner.

But that wasn't good enough. I needed to enter their world for the afternoon, they said in so many words. I needed to join them in a good rousing game of laser tag.

I couldn't.

"Come on!" said Jimmy. "This is quality time spent with your sons. And you'll love it. It's just like playing capture the flag or kickball."

The boys snorted in disbelief.

"Yeah, right," they said.

So they propelled me into the car, and we headed for Austin. In the back seat, the hormones raged. Strategies for killing with a single point of light were passed back and forth as if the boys had turned into warlords. I shrank further down into the front seat and turned up the Scottish music, hoping the heather and the fiddles would drown out the end of the world being plotted in the back seat.

I tried to remember what I had liked to do as a girl beset by hormones, and I conjured up a dim vision of myself at the neighborhood drug store makeup counter with my girlfriends, sampling the latest, palest shade of lipstick. Rose on Ice was my pallor of choice and Shalimar my fragrance. We must have looked like the walking dead with our long, straight hair, our pale lips, and our blue mascara, but we thought we were beautiful, exotic even, and perhaps ...

"Mom! We're there!"

And we were. After circling Highland Mall five or six times, we had finally found Laser Quest, and all the languid pallor and the Shalimar of the late '60s gave way to a minor nightmare.

"Why don't I just wait here for you, guys?" I said sweetly. "I really can't play laser tag. I'm a girl."

They snorted again.

"Yeah, right, Mom! You think girls can't play laser tag? Girls play laser tag all the time!"

"But do they like it?" I asked.

"Yes, Mom. They like it. They like it a lot."

"But I don't like killing people," I tried.

More snorts.

"You don't actually kill them, Mom. It's a game."

I could see that I wasn't putting my best foot forward in the mother-son bonding scheme of things, so I ascended from the car and began the long walk across the parking lot of the mall.

I should also mention here that I am not big on malls. Probably I am an anachronism in the blaze of this acquisitive economy, but malls are filled with too many choices, so many, in fact, that I seldom go, opting to stay home and not buy anything instead.

So here I was, walking across the mall parking lot toward the war zone, my boys bouncing alongside like Tigger and Roo, Jimmy and his fifteen-year-old towering over all of us, all of us ready to conquer the world with our swords of light.

Inside, the teenagers swarmed. Birthday parties bloomed in the lobby's side rooms, and a young man threw up at my feet as I walked in the door.

"This is a bad omen," I said, feeling very weary indeed. "The game has made that child sick. It's the violence factor. I don't think I can take it."

"Come on, Mom. You'll be fine."

At the counter, the clerk asked me for my code name. Code name? Linda won't do?

"Ask them first," I mumbled, gesturing to the kids while desperately floundering in my mind for a code name that would somehow empower me with machismo and warlike grace.

I glanced at the video screens boasting the latest scores and saw names like PsychoMike and PsychoDude and ... "Irish," I said. "I'll be Irish."

The clerk frowned, shrugged, and coded me in as Irish.

"Irish," said Jimmy, who was going by the code name Excalibur. "I like that."

"Irish?" said the boys. "Irish?"

Bards, I thought. *Poets and storytellers. Lovers and leprechauns, singers and harpists.* "Irish."

"Okay, Mom. Whatever."

"Look," said Jimmy. "These are your adversaries. These are the people you're trying to kill. These are the people who will be killing you with their lasers."

I looked around at the adolescent crowd and the one father with a small, frightened boy in tow and a smaller, clueless boy on his shoulders.

"Cool," I murmured. "Way cool."

Then suddenly we're all in a room together, and a muscular, heavy blond young woman is barking orders at us in warrior fashion, spewing the words out so fast they pelt us like machine gun fire.

"Could you slow down?" I begged. "I can't understand you."

"I have to talk this fast so we don't run off schedule," she says, but she slows down, even comes to a dead stop when the swarming kids won't stop talking. She's tough and she's mean and she makes us all swear an oath that we won't "run, gang up on each other, cuss, or behave irresponsibly."

I snort in disbelief. I may not be a warrior yet, but I know that all's fair in love and war, and I'm beginning to think I'm the only lover in this bunch.

I'm also the only one in sandals, and it occurs to me as she herds us into a black room with flashing black strobe lights that sandals are not very warriorlike.

"It's okay, Mom," whispers one of my children. "I won't shoot you very much."

"Thanks," I whisper back, wondering if that's kind of like ganging up, which we're not supposed to do.

The blonde instructs us on where to aim in order to kill each other, and we don these hulking black harnesses that carry our vulnerable spots and our weapon. I pass my key over my laser gun, and it says, "Welcome, Irish."

And then we're in the maelstrom of strobes and smoke and flashing red lasers and we're all trying to kill each other and I shoot wildly at anything that moves as I feel my vest buzz every ten seconds to tell me I've been shot.

Warriors are running and ganging up, and "Jumpin' Jack Flash" by the Stones is hammering in the background as I maneuver the maze-like black walls, lit only by mirrors and winking lasers and flashing lights.

My youngest son, Squirtl, rounds the corner and offs me, yelling, "Gotcha, Mom! Isn't this fun?"

I hum a few bars of one of my favorite songs, "Get Together," and back into a corner until my vest stops vibrating. "C'mon people now, Smile on your brother . . ."

Zap! Wrong song. I'm vibrating again. I bump into Jimmy in the dark. He doesn't even kiss me, but he doesn't kill me, either. Lasers bounce from mirrors, and I vibrate. They're running. They're ganging up. I fall down and bust my knees. Wrong footgear, sandals, for a warrior. Someone named CowGirl laughs and zings me with her laser. "Jumpin' Jack Flash is a gas! Gas! Gas!"

I think I'm getting the hang of it. Aim at the lights on their harnesses. Hug the walls. Stay away from grates and mirrors. Don't fall down.

And it's over. The girl warriors (who ganged up) are giggling. The guy warriors are beating their chests and boasting. We haul our harnesses over our heads and exit the black, smoky pit. Everyone's coughing.

"Wasn't that fun, Mom? Didn't you love it?"

And then the results are up on the video screen, and I and the rest of the world can see in black in white that I am no warrior. I would be the first to go down in wartime. I don't have the competitive edge. I don't love the conflict.

My oldest son scored seventh out of a field of twenty-eight players, with 444 points. I had scored twenty-seventh, with 10 points. I think number twenty-eight was the boy riding on his father's shoulders. My boys are laughing. They are jubilant. They are high with the warrior spirit. They live and relive the last twenty minutes.

I watch their sparkling eyes, and I worry a little about this crazed pastime.

But they are kind. They put their arms around me. They tell me I'll do better next time. At least I didn't get a negative score.

Next time? I balk.

"Hey, boys," I say. "Want to go hang out at the makeup counter?"

Death of a Spring

If I were the man you wanted,
I would not be the man that I am.
— LYLE LOVETT

So go the words to a clever country song, but how true, I think, as I steel my nerves to the whining of the bulldozer and the dump truck across the creek. How often we try to change the nature of the thing we love.

I was a lucky child. Each summer, my parents loaded us into the station wagon and hauled us across the deserts from California to Wimberley. After the long, arid stretches of Arizona and New Mexico, Wimberley seemed a tangled piece of heaven.

It was green and lush, even in the heat of summer. Grapevine looped and wove itself through the cypress, whole fields tumbled before me in horsemint and gallardia, and even the bull nettle seemed a dangerous, stickery beauty.

The Blanco River was a dream of easy floating, of sunlight and stark white cliffs softened in cypress and nameless vines and maidenhair fern. Cypress Creek was all cool blue wonder. It was rope swings and waterfalls and cypress knees and quicksilver fish. And all around the water, the green tumbled and tangled and braided itself into the trees and the rocks and the wild and native shrubs.

There was such a wilderness to it all, to the water and the land, a wilderness that I could not claim in the pretty piece of California suburbia from which we had driven away. As a child, I loved it, stood in awe of it. As an adult, I crave it.

In a world where we strive for a disciplined order to govern our overflowing lives, where computers control our destinies, where virtual reality is replacing the world it mimics, I crave a piece of wildness that thrives beyond my efforts, that grows effortlessly upward, like the racy, wild climb of the mustang grape. I crave the song of tiny tree frogs hidden in the leaves at night, the study in stillness of the great blue heron who fishes beneath my window in the mornings and soars, with his mate, through the feathered tunnel of cypress along the creek. I crave the uninterrupted starlight, the black, hollow beauty of the moonless night. I need to wake to the canyon wren's descending scale.

This weekend, I awoke to bulldozers.

Across the creek from me was once a small pocket of wetland, marshland, soggy ground surrounding a healthy natural spring. It was home to the tree frogs and tender shoots of miner's lettuce. It squished beneath my feet when I ventured its edge, and probably housed a host of undesirables, like sinewy, dangerous water snakes and several varieties of man-eating mosquitoes.

But it was beautiful in its lack of artifice. It held beneath its spongy surface an abundance of generous water. It offered an untouched habitat and an earthy, wet fragrance of green and growing things.

It's mostly gone now. After the big machines have left, the small marshland has become a flattened, cleared-out field of dirt upon which will be sown a lawn, a gentle green slide of park-like carpet grass to welcome its owners to the banks of the creek. The spring is still there. Its small, placid pool is stronger than it looks and would withstand most attempts to fill it in, so the owners of the land appear to have left it, but the marshlands surrounding it are gone.

It's been a tough weekend, listening to the bulldozer and the dump truck do their county-sanctioned clearing of the land, and it has raised a textbook's worth of questions for me. They are not particularly profound or innovative questions. They've been asked before, and they've been answered through action. So perhaps with the disappearance of the swamp across the creek, I am simply mourning an inevitable change.

Most of us moved here from somewhere else because we craved that element of wildness. Wimberley has always meant freedom, even to the first settlers who found it was not an agricultural heaven and didn't have soil deep enough to grow the grass to feed the cattle. It didn't matter. This valley was so generous with what it had and opened its wide arms to so many people that now we are losing the intrinsic beauty that lured us here to begin with.

We have been a steady stream of inhabitants, we settlers—for that is what we still are, even if our saddlebags now hold laptops and cellular phones. Like those who came before, we carve our niche of land from the wild, and we tame it to meet our needs. It's just that now, so many of us have come and imposed our will on the delicate beauty that we love that we are carving the spirit from her soul.

You've seen it happen. You've seen the love affairs, the great passions, where the stronger of the two takes the cherished other and proceeds to polish and perfect until the other's beauty is replaced with artifice and makeovers, and the heart of the passion has stilled to boredom or to the small, whining voice of disappointment. It happens all the time, and it makes no sense. Hence, the song.

But the land cannot fight back as well. The language it speaks is becoming archaic, a predecessor to Latin, a tongue we don't hear much anymore. Its profound simplicity doesn't meet our current needs, and we impose our own pictures on a landscape that we are in danger of forgetting we ever loved.

We see water, and we see many lots along the bank, so we build many houses very close. We envision manicured parklands, so we clear the joyous, rambling green and fill in the low spots and move the big rocks until all is a uniform and tended green. We dig our wells a little deeper because we need a little longer straw to reach that water so vital to the carpet grass. We manicure and we create what we left behind when we moved here. We wipe out the tiny marshes.

Last year, it was bulldozers and floating ashes from across the river as they flattened and burned the wild tangle along the riverbank for a large development. Now the riverbank recedes from the knees of the cypress because the land is eroding without its safety net of roots and native green to hold it true.

But that's the way it is, it seems. Someone's going to do it, I've heard. Someone's going to break up the swell and roll of the land. Could be a lot worse.

How we tear at what we love. How we reshape the beauty we so crave. How we ruin the best designs of all.

The big machines aren't here today, and, soon, I suspect the newly laid topsoil will be thatched with carpet grass and we will see a continuous roll of uninterrupted green sprawled across from us. Children will play on its slope. Lawn parties will grace its spread. It will be pretty and cool. Change is inevitable. I will grow accustomed.

But for now I harbor a silent and furious grief. The song of destruction is a hard melody to awaken one on a soft, summer morning. I grieve the passing of the natural. I grieve the taming of the wild beauty inside us all.

Rain Song

An Indian Rain Song

Killi killi killi killi watch watch watch watch
Kay you kin kum kawa
killi killi killi killi watch watch watch watch
Kay you kin kum kawa
I yama chama
I chama pollywama
I yama chama
I chama pollywa!

Killi killi killi killi watch watch watch watch
Kay you kin kum kawa
Killi killi killi killi watch watch watch watch
Kay you kin kum kawa
I yama chama
I chama pollywama
I yama chama
I chama pollywa!

Killi killi ...

And so on until it rains. You don't believe me? A little skeptical? I know all about skepticism. It has worn an unreasonable hole in my heart that leaks belief like an aging cistern.

But I believe in the rain song.

Remember those scattered showers we had last Monday? Remember how the clouds gathered, and the air grew musty with the smell of moisture? And then—at least in some parts of town—that rare commodity known as rain spattered itself across the dusty windshields of cars and the hard-pack of dirt roads. It ran down rain gutters, some new enough to be virgin to that flowing water, and spilled into parking lots. It made me wonder where I had put my umbrella, just in case I needed it.

I didn't. The rain stopped just in time to be a good tease, an appetizer savory enough to leave you wishing you'd ordered two.

But do you know where that rain came from? It wasn't in the forecast. It just sort of appeared, tilted the pitcher and streamed down for a bit until the pitcher was empty.

I think I know where that rain came from. Saturday night, the Wimberley Institute of Cultures held their annual River Blessing, this time on Cypress Creek at Scudder's, a deep green pool of a swimming hole, encircled in cypress and rope swings and shored up by a small and very old dam.

More than a hundred people attended the event, and I wasn't one of them, although my children were able to work it into their schedules. In fact, they and their grandfather, Jack Williams, were featured on the program.

Organizer Kay Henderson had heard that my father had a potent song that he sang in times of drought, a kind of cure-all pill for the ravages of unrelenting heat, and she asked him to sing it at the blessing.

Knowing that all prayers—and song is prayer—are best received when buoyed by belief in numbers, my father asked my children to sing with him.

Malone, at ten, is the skeptic's skeptic. Scientific by nature, he questions even the most basic of life's procedures and takes them very seriously. He isn't given to spontaneous song and thinks that silliness is silliness. Much of his life these days is spent organizing and reorganizing his Beanie Baby collection. I watch the process and understand that he is seeking the meaning of order in the universe on a microcosmic level.

Cameron, at seven, is willing to believe in anything and laughs so loud that I have to urge discretion. He sings before the hat is dropped and performs without a stage. Much of his life these days is spent losing his Beanie Baby collection, his shoes, his socks, anything not directly attached to his body. I watch the process and understand that he is seeking the continuity of life inherent in chaos on any level.

My father learned the rain song as a boy at Camp Tom Wooten. Some of his friends maintain that it is a Camp Tom Wooten song, but my father swears it is a Kiowa rain song, and we used to sing it all along the arid stretches of Arizona and New Mexico as we made our pilgrimage from California to Texas and back each summer.

When you sing the rain song, repetition is the key. You have to sing it over and over and over and over again until people beg you to stop, and then you politely acknowledge their pleas with a smile and a nod — if you are well bred — and keep singing. Otherwise, you simply ignore them and keep singing. One verse won't do it. You must sing it over and over and over and over again.

Repetition is a key to many religions. Repetition is a key to the force of belief.

As we drove across those deserts shimmering in the lovely, dry lies of water, as we watched mesa after mesa loom and recede, as we passed trading posts and gas stations that sold you batteries you didn't need and filled your tank with silty fuel, we sang the rain song:

"Killi killi killi killi watch watch watch watch / kay you kin kum kawa ..." and so on and so forth. And always, it seemed, we could feel the sky collecting itself, hunching its ponderous shoulders for a low, guttural growl. The desert sky deepened into purple clouds that gathered against the level tops of the mesas. Shards of light would rip that dark, soft cotton, and the rain would descend in the lessening distance like gray scarves caught in a grayer wind. The blond sands would deepen to a blackened gold.

We would drive into the rain and rejoice in the proof of our beliefs, which, fed since we were babies, we never doubted. The Kiowa rain song brought rain, and that was all there was to it. Getting other people to believe was difficult at times, but there's nothing that diminishes doubt like the outcome of belief.

I think we all want to believe. We want to raise our voices in supplication that is both song and hope. And we want to be answered. It doesn't matter the language from which the words are carved if they correspond to the language of the heart, and anyone who has ever prayed for rain knows that the subtext of the words they use is the fervent beating of the heart.

A few years ago when drought seared these hillsides, my father taught my sweetheart the words to the song, and the two of them sang it independently and together. Jimmy sang it driving back and forth from Wimberley to Martindale, where he lived, and when the rains broke, they followed his course, starting north of Wimberley and drying out in Martindale. The weatherman was perplexed. He hadn't foreseen the rain, he said. He could only tell you it rained and the path the rain took. He just couldn't figure it out. We could.

And then there was the other night. My father stood between my two sons, and the three of them, accompanied by Jim Henderson's soft guitar, sang that rain song over and over and over again for the WIC crowd, who were well fed and ready for rain.

Malone stood solemn and intent, skeptical to the bone but willing to please. My father stood in the middle as the leader of the chorus and urged the voices of the audience to join him, and Cameron, who was dancing like a water sprite on the dam when his stage call came, raced to the microphone, shoeless and wet, just in time to sing. According to all reports, he accompanied the rain song with a rain dance, an innovation all his own.

My father says he could hear voices joining him after several repetitions, and the crowd was amiable. "Whatever works" seemed to be the aura of the day.

Well, it worked. I'm not saying it couldn't work better, but you have to start somewhere. Some folks in Wimberley never saw the rain that fell last Monday, but some reveled in it. And my parents received quite a few phone calls, several of which started out, "I believe. I believe." Some people asked for the words to the song, and I think my father may have sung it over the phone a time or two to refresh memories.

But it worked!

I don't know what anchors some beliefs and not others. I don't know what makes the impossible possible, what sways the wind to change, but I believe in the repetition of belief and the prayers that manifest themselves in song. I believe in ancient faith—even if it did come from Camp Tom Wooten. I believe in the rain song.

Shooting Stars

I have always wanted to see a meteor shower. I love fireworks—the bright, blinding fountains of light, and I have
thought that a meteor shower might be an unending show of ar-
rows blazing through the sky.

But until the other night, I have always been disappointed. I
was becoming an unbeliever.

Texas is a wonderful land for falling stars. Our Hill Country
has a sky that won't stop, that stretches the horizon at night to
make room for the billions of stars that swell their dark space
and pulse like distant drumbeats.

When I was a child, I would lie, summer nights, on army
blankets stretched across my grandmother's lawn in San
Marcos. She would point out the constellations, and my throat
would fill with the need to cry over something so profound it
had no name.

When the streetlights finally paraded down her street, she
brought the army blankets with her when she came to
Wimberley, and we would lie in the clearing above the riverbank, surrounded by pecan trees and chiggers, and we would
talk in whispers, as if the stars would be distracted by our
words.

Sometimes in that stillness, we would see a brilliant slash.
We would see the black void split apart as a fault of light ripped
through the sky, and, for a brief second, just long enough to

gasp, the statues of the stars would stand aside for the racehorse in their midst.

We would suck in our breath and squeeze hands. "Did you see it?" we would cry. "Did you see the shooting star?"

We would count those bright white slashes, and we would lie for what seemed like hours watching the motionless sky for more.

I remember sneaking out of my cabin at camp and spreading sleeping bags in the fields of Johnson grass above the Guadalupe River. My friends and I would lie like secrets in the fields and gaze intently at the night sky. We were stealthy and powerful with the knowledge that we were not supposed to be lying in the fields, that we were supposed to be dreaming in our bunks, locked in the darkness of sleep, while, instead, we were telling lies and truths to the impenetrable sky, pocked with the light of stars.

Something in that scattered light loosens the reluctant tongue, spreads the secrets like a low-lying fog, and builds and strengthens dreams. We would imagine our lives on those nights—who we would become and how. We would will the wishes of our hearts into the bright dust of shooting stars—and there were always a few—because we knew that in the insomnia of starlight, anything is possible.

And then, some of us would grow quieter, and we would realize we were forgetting our secrets as we slipped into sleep, giving them away to the stars. So we would shake the sleepy ones softly, gather up the sleeping bags, and tiptoe back through the grass and burrs to the cabins, mostly successful, we thought, in our brief escapes.

I think now the counselors may have known, may have lay quietly in their bunks and watched our shadows move down the bunk-bed ladders, out the screen door, and across the big lawns. They probably watched the subtle play of our flashlights, searching out the fields, watched us stumble back in and up the ladders. And they never said a word.

In the morning, we would wake covered with red welts from the chigger bites. I remember the waterfront counselors staring at us in our two-piece swimsuits, wondering what rare disease we had contracted during the night. They wouldn't let us in the chill, clear waters of the Guadalupe, and we, of course, could not tell them of the night we had spent feasting on starlight while the chiggers feasted on us. So, we spent the morning in the infirmary and painted the welts with clear nail polish and slept.

Maybe some of the wishes came true. By the time they did, we had probably moved on to others and forgotten we had made them.

In college, I took astronomy. Given to words and theater lights, I had a strong aversion to anything as concrete as math or science. There was no give and take in numbers, or if there was, it always resulted in the wrong answer. Science seemed to harbor a little more mystery, a little more room to move in, but not much. There were still a few things out there that hadn't been figured out yet, and the ones that had been figured out were described in words, not numbers, so I took as much science as I could to fulfill the math and science requirement of my liberal arts degree.

After I had made my way through the anthropology department and ground my way through geology in deference to my geologist brother, I decided I would study the stars for a semester.

Stars were poetry and vastness. Stars were half real and half dream. In winter skies, they were sharp, broken pieces of frozen glass. They were icy air breathed in. They were the bubbles in tall, clear champagne flutes. In summer skies, the ice melted to softened edges and lights as white as the legends of childhood. They held up the sky. They cast a more compelling spell than any theater light.

And if one should chance to fall, you could catch it forever in memory because no one ever forgets a falling star.

I would take astronomy and learn the mystery of the skies. I was actually excited by the idea until I found out that the science of astronomy is numbers. What I had yearned for was the romance, which my aged professor explained to all 300 of us in the lecture hall, was inane drivel. This was a science class, and we would learn no astrology, myth, or history during the next several months. We would not speculate about extraterrestrial goings-on, and we would memorize distances and circumferences and names. A few times at night, if the skies were cloudless, we would be invited to peer through the cold rim of the university's telescope and draw a picture of what we saw, but there were to be no aliens in the portrait.

Sadly, I remember little from the class except for the evenings spent huddled around the telescope, trying to describe the magnificence that surrounded Saturn with weak circles drawn in pencil. A few of the constellations stayed with me, and I can always find the Seven Sisters in the sky.

I did learn, however, that August is a good time for meteor showers, and I set up my first meteor-watching party on the banks of the Blanco River, following a picnic dinner. My relatives and friends attended, certain I knew what I was talking about because I had just completed a course in astronomy, and everyone knew I was a good student.

After a full meal, we lay back on the hard white limestone and waited for it to get dark. In the summer, true darkness often comes later than we think. It seemed to get darker later than usual that August night, the twilight lingering at the edges of the sky, as if it, too, would wait around for the falling-star exhibition.

Finally the dark settled in, like a dog turning circles in the dirt until the right moment calls for it to lie down and sleep. We lay there—all of us—much as I had when I was a child with my grandmother, and we waited for God's fireworks to begin. And we waited. We talked a little, and we waited and waited and waited. Someone started snoring. I felt like I had invited everyone to my favorite restaurant, and the food had arrived cold or not at all. I felt like the emperor walking naked down the street after his people have discovered he has no clothes.

Maybe we saw one shooting star—not even big enough to pin your life's hopes on. Maybe we didn't. I remember that evening as being long and anticlimactic. And embarrassing. After a few polite hours, my friends and relatives nodded to the stars, prodded the snorer with their foot, folded up their blankets, and went home.

So did I.

Ahh, well. I read the next morning that the stars had fallen around 3 A.M. So be it. We were not supposed to see them.

Years later, I led friends on a trek up Mount Baldy to see the tail of Haley's Comet, but the clouds soaked in any light like blotter paper, so we drank beer and talked about what we thought it might look like if we could see it.

Several months ago, I sat with my boys and my sweetheart on the deck at nightfall, snapping green beans and hoping to catch the Draconid showers. I had learned by then to harness my expectations. Expect too much of the world, and it will hunker away in shame. Look at it out of the corner of your eye, and you might see something. I thought the bushel of green beans might be a good distraction for the stars, give them room to play and race through the heavens like my children race through my living room, but they didn't. They knew the beans were a ruse, and they sulked and stood in the sky like stone.

So when the papers predicted a fireworks display with the Leonid showers earlier this month, I almost missed it. I figured the emperor's clothes were not only nonexistent, but their fabled transparency was becoming threadbare, as well. I would not wake up at 4 A.M. on a cold November morning and gear up in some semblance of warmth and stare at the motionless sky. Much as I love the stars—and, oh, I love the stars—I am nobody's fool. Besides, I have more wishes these days than a fireworks display could ever begin to resolve.

So I got up at 4 A.M. and threw a jacket over my flannel gown and slipped shoes on bare feet, and ran outside for a view of the western sky. My sweetheart came along, and we promised each other we would only stay a minute or two, and then we would go back to bed if we saw no action. It was too late and too early for dallying with hope.

And then we saw one like a snowy flash across the sky. And then we saw another and another and another and I ran inside and called to my children that the stars were falling and grabbed blankets and they ran outside with us dressed in clothes ten sizes too big and we all lay on lawn chairs and watched the most beautiful fireworks I have ever seen.

God has such incredible timing. We never lost interest, and we stopped counting the traveling lights. I felt like crying and squeezed my oldest son every time I saw a star fall.

"Mom," he said. "Why are you squeezing me?"

"Because I love the stars," I said, *And because I love you*, I

thought. And because I have waited all my life to see this wonderment. And it's not numbers. And it is mysterious. And it's real.

In between stars—and there wasn't much in-between—we talked about the stupid airplanes that moved like lantern-bearing snails through the sky.

("There's another stupid plane."

"They're not stupid. That's thousands of tons of steel up there in the sky. How do you think they fly?"

"They have pilots."

Pause. Shooting star or two. Then—

"There's another stupid plane."

"They're not stupid ..."

"I know, I know. They have pilots.")

We talked about what they were, those beautiful lights. How they were the frozen dust of a comet's tail—which only reinforces my idea that all the dust in this world never goes away, only gets rearranged. Ahhh, but what a beautiful composition of dust.

The stars went on until I remembered the children had school in the morning, and I had a life. We decided to count to thirty, and if no stars had fallen, we would leave, but they fell and fell and fell. We never could make it to thirty. I even quit wishing. I figure greed will get you nowhere, and beauty only multiplies the more you simply leave it be.

They were so beautiful, those stars. And we had nothing to do with their beauty. It was a show we were privileged to watch, a dazzling symphony of light and silence. Powerlessness has never felt so freeing.

I believe in meteor showers again. That night seems surreal now—the beauty, the conversations, the young voices, the laughter, the silence.

What a gift in the darkness. If God is pure light, as some people believe, he was signing the skies in cursive that night.

I don't save autographs, but I'm saving that one.

Memory

The bones of memory are not
the hollow bones of flight
or the sullen, solid fossils of the grave.
But rather they are supple,
bend, in dance, to music,
a making of the music of the life.

At night, the body sleeps, draped
in shadows, swallowed
by the holes in the light.
A child who is simple beyond
the simple knowing
stands at the edge of shade and light
and goes no farther.
He tests the air beyond him
with his foot laced in shoes he cannot tie,
but will not make the step
toward the darker light.
Father, he cries, his voice
a fluted high note
in the dying summer air—
Father, come and help me.

Father, there are holes in the light.

The attendant crowd,
the uncles and the aunts
and the tiny, wayward cousins,
laugh, a spattered percussion,
a rain of broken glass.
The boy stands poised
in a vision all his own
against the backdrop of the laughter,
and the laughter
lives forever
like a slippery kind of music
in the bone.

I remember how the father
doesn't laugh but
stoops to touch the child
and tilts the smaller face
to meet his face
so that the eyes are filled with light.
It's only shadow, Ben, he says,
and lifts the boy from sun to shadow
and back again to sun.
He hums a tuneless, timeless song.
He holds those glowing bones
against his own.

The holes in the light are where
we sleep, where
we lose ourselves in shadows
and dream a rhythmless parade
of blackened notes
against a whiter page.
Memory bends backward on itself,
a rubber circle where the ends don't meet.

mber is not
ened, but the flexing
one, a small, dark music,
eate ourselves
no we will become,
one.

FORCEFUL INTENT

A PORTER NOVEL

R.A. MCGEE

DAREWOOD
PRESS